# BUTTERFLY TRANSITION

# BUTTERFLY TRANSITION

A Step-by-Step Guide to Transitioning Your Hair
While Growing Through Life's Changes

*Diana Ramsey*

Forward by Felicia Leatherwood

Published by SistersWithBeauty
First Paperback Edition

Cover photography by E.Y.E Imagery Studio
Book cover design & concept by Julian B. Kiganda
Interior graphic by Dana Bly of Pardon My Fro
Interior book design by Najat Haynes
Book editing by Candice L. Davis

This book is available for special promotions, corporate training or bulk pricing. For details, contact books@sisterswithbeauty.com.

## See What People Are Saying About
# BUTTERFLY TRANSITION

"With hard-won expertise, the author guides readers to customize and simplify their natural hair care routine. At the same time, she tells her own story of personal growth with an authenticity and openness that makes readers feel like they've reunited with an old friend. This book is a vital resource for women who yearn to live life by their own rules and choose to love themselves while they do so."

—*Candice L Davis of* GoWriteSomething.com

"Each chapter pulls back more layers of her courage, determination, and vulnerability. This book, her hair transition, felt like part of my own story and experiences. I laughed, I cried, I smiled. Well worth the read. Bravo my beautiful sister!"

—*Georgette Pierre of* GeorgettePierre.com

"The book I wish I had when I was transitioning from relaxing my hair to wearing my natural texture."

—*Jonna Scott-Blakes of* Naturally-Glam.com

"Diana's transparency about her own natural hair journey made me reflect on my own relationship with my hair and has empowered me to find strength in my own truth. This book is not just for people that are transitioning back to their natural hair, it's for anyone transitioning in life. It will encourage you to keep on growing."

—*Ronnie Tyler of* BlackandMarriedWithKids.com

"Diana Ramsey's Butterfly Transition is a step-by-step guidebook that features an easy-to-follow plan that guides you through the physical, emotional, and spiritual phases of returning to natural. Use this book to normalize the often unfamiliar and uncertain process of transitioning!"

—*Seanna-Kaye & Shalleen-Kaye of* NaturalHairDoesCare.com

# BUTTERFLY DEDICATION

*To my truth,*
*may it free more than just me.*

# ACKNOWLEDGMENTS

The best gift anyone can ever give you is wings. Wings allow one to reach higher achievements, endeavors, and dreams.

The team on the *Butterfly Transition* project not only gifted me wings, but they carried me when I forgot how to fly. Mom, Jessica, Julian, Danni, Crystale, Yoko, Lesley, T. Espi, Tameka, Najat, Candice, and Markus (the only man on the project); the work you did on the *Butterfly Transition* project will never go unnoticed or unstated.

Thank you for sharing your gifts with me. Thank you for shining your light on me so that I may feel the rays and shine on. I am because you are, and I will always be thankful for your gift of wings.

# CONTENTS

# FOREWORD

The encouragement, enlightenment, and humor of *Butterfly Transition* have touched my soul in a way that makes me reflect on my childhood and some of the choices I have made with my own hair and in my life as a whole.

I truly enjoyed reading the details of author Diana Ramsey's life journey to understand her hair, along with the great natural beauty secrets and hair rituals she shares throughout the book. Together, they will cause you to reflect on your own relationship with your hair and help you learn how to love your tresses.

I love how Diana Ramsey expresses how she learned to develop her own unique techniques for appreciating her hair and her life as fully expressed through her hair.

This book belongs to the new and old generations of naturalistas and also serves as a perfect guide to new naturals, encouraging them to embrace their own textures. The reflections of Diana's younger years are expressed in a way that brings me back to my childhood hair neglect and are priceless because Diana's stories are so colorful and vivid.

Reading each chapter of this book helped me gain a new appreciation for where I am as a natural today, and I truly feel that a lot of women will be using this book as a great template to guide themselves through the world of natural hair styling and products.

This book is self-transformative, and the process that you allow to happen while associating with the stories of life and love by way of hair will open you up to seeing what it is you really hold true about yourself as it relates to your hair. What thoughts have you experienced while transitioning into a butterfly? How well are you treating yourself through the transition?

As a hairstylist for well over twenty years now, I definitely can say that this is a great book to guide you to liking and loving your return to being a naturalista. I really hope that you take the time to allow Diana to guide you into your full expression of beauty and love.

You will not be disappointed with this transformational return to love with your beautiful butterfly natural hair!

Felicia M. Leatherwood

# PREFACE

I never expected making a decision to change the way I cared for my hair would show me a parallel reflection of my life. There was a relationship between my hair and life transitions, but I quieted the urge to talk about it. There was no doubt I cared about my natural hair, but my life waited on the sidelines in need of that same consideration. I'm just like my hair, still growing, stretching, extending, and coming into my own.

I've gone through struggles, triumphs, setbacks, and experiences in my life as I have experienced the same with my hair. Standing firm in my understanding that *Butterfly Transition* couldn't only be about hair is what kept me awake at night, writing feverishly. Writing about transitions has helped me break free from the hold my hair and my life experiences have had on me.

We all deserve to be free from anything that pushes us into a smaller existence than the one intended for us. It's in these pages that I hope to set my hair and my life free with my own truth. In reading this book, may you find your way through your own hair and life transitions.

"It is in our own truth that we set ourselves free."

—DIANA RAMSEY

# 1 | My Hair Story

It's taken me five years of my natural hair journey to finally give my hair the credit it deserves for its role in saving my life.

Like many Black women, I've spent more of my life relaxed than I have being natural; over twenty-four years to be exact, but who's counting? My hair story is similar to yours—scalp burns, scabs, touch-ups, burned hair, neutralizing shampoo, petroleum on my edges, and letting the relaxer sit another five minutes too long.

Isn't that *the Black Girl Hair Story*? If it wasn't your hair story as a child, somehow, someway relaxers found you. I was seven years old when I was first introduced to relaxers, so my choice in the matter didn't really exist. I kept up with the tradition.

I am the youngest of three girls, born in Chicago, Illinois, and raised in Riverside, California. My mother was our kitchen beautician, styling my two older sisters' hair and mine all kinds of ways. I remember one particular style my mom did, which was my first full sew-in. Later, looking back at family photos made me realize we all in some way resembled Rick James with the hair my mom selected, but when I say this in front of her, she instantly gets mad. I think she believes it paints a negative picture of her. There is one thing a black mother won't stand for, and that's someone implying her children looked crazy on purpose.

After I'd worn the style long enough, my mother appointed my middle oldest sister to remove my sew-in. But something didn't go as planned. As my sister cut the sew-in thread from my head, she soon realized she had cut portions of my real hair during the removal process.

Mom was furious, and I remember feeling sad, like something had been taken away from me that I couldn't get back. It wasn't as if my sister intentionally cut my hair off (if she did, she kept a great poker face), but it happened. The emotions from that moment shaped my perception of how society viewed short hair as compared to long hair. I was only seven, but I could see the importance and beauty expectations that were placed on having long hair.

The impression long hair made on me at an early age was embedded from that moment. I didn't have long hair, and as a child growing up, this was the first real difference I noticed between my middle oldest sister and me. Hair length was important in the Black community. Long hair was paraded like a badge of honor, almost to demonstrate your mother knew what she was doing with your upkeep and care. I saw how family members and strangers complimented my mother because of my sister's long hair. I wanted to be just like my sister and receive the same credit little black girls with long hair got. It was as if you did something right without trying and everyone praised you for it.

But I was the little black girl with average-growing hair, the type of hair length that didn't receive many compliments. I got the same hairstyle as my sister, but it never looked the same and left me feeling different about how I viewed myself. My mother would have to modify my sister's style because of her length, and I would watch, saying, "Long hair gets all the attention." It seems a bit crazy to consider this idea as an adult, but as a child it was the only conclusion that made sense. Long hair was special, and because my hair would barely grow past my chin, I grew up thinking my hair wasn't special. This conclusion, at such a young age, followed me into adulthood. My mother instilled in me the importance of taking care of and loving myself. I added my own emphasis on keeping my hair perfect so all would admire it. My hairstyles became the only way I could separate myself from how inadequate not having long hair made me feel.

I accepted my childhood lesson of wearing amazing hairstyles as my consolation prize for not being born with long hair. My quest to remain fly from every hair follicle led me to horrible hair decisions, such as coloring and relaxing my hair at the same time. I never wore the same style twice, ever. My need to have the best hairstyle masked the hurt of wanting long hair. I remember placing towels or a T-shirt on my head, trying to create the image of long hair in my own make-believe world. Imagining that if I had been born lucky enough to have long hair, my life would somehow be different.

Something as simple as hair length pushed me to always change my look with weave, color, cuts, and fresh relaxers just to get the same admiration I grew up seeing my sister receive. I had opted to live in my own compliment box, where I could control the feelings people experienced when they saw my hair. I thought I could control the thoughts others had by keeping their attention on styles set to pique their full appreciation. Hearing compliments like "Girl, you stay with a fly hairstyle" became my fix, and I got high off the recognition. It boosted every ounce of my confidence.

I navigated life with a relaxer all the way through college. I attended a Historically Black College and University (HBCU) at Norfolk State University (class of 2006). I was in class with girls who looked different and managed their hair just the same. Many were natural, and there was an array of diversity in styles, looks, and attire. But the natural girls on campus didn't inspire me to return to natural hair. Their fros, coils, and curls didn't have anything to do with me getting my Vital relaxer from my college beautician.

It wasn't until I graduated and accepted an internship with the federal government, in the Washington, DC, metropolitan area, that I decided to return to my natural hair. I simply told myself I wasn't going to relax my hair anymore; it was just that simple. I didn't read any books to help me along the way, and I didn't know the first thing about washing or caring for my hair. While I found my lack of knowledge sad, I still did nothing to change it. I was accustomed to using hairstyles as my way of showing I actually cared about myself.

I went into my first natural hair attempt totally blind and uneducated. As I approached the eighth month of my hair transition, I still wasn't educating myself. After I experienced a bad hair washing that left my hair matted on top of my head, I gave in and relaxed my hair again. In hindsight, I wasn't returning to anything because I hadn't tried to educate myself before embarking on my journey. I had decided to not use relaxers, but I failed to make any type of plan on what to do after I made that decision. My reaction after failing at managing my natural hair was to return to relaxers. Relaxers had been there as my follicle friend for over twenty-four years, keeping me straight (pun intended).

The idea to return to my natural hair resurfaced when I accepted a job in San Antonio, Texas. I took the new job to get away from life as I knew it in Northern Virginia. I was in need of a life change. Things had become very boring, and I wanted to get away from what others thought of me, but really what I thought of myself. My network was my comfort zone on the East Coast. I had achieved a great-paying government job, my own fully furnished apartment, a new car, and all of the ideals of what it looked like to be young, black, and free. But I wasn't fulfilled, and if I can be honest with you, I wasn't very happy.

When the opportunity presented itself for me to move to a state where no one knew my name, I found it to be both freeing and necessary. I wanted to know I could make it without all the people I had come to lean and depend on. In this moment, I started to test my idea of being able to make it anywhere in this world. This was the moment my hair and my life got packed up and we all moved to another state.

Upon arriving in Texas, I decided to return to my natural hair, again. Over five years had passed since my first attempt, and the second time around, I knew what I had done wrong before. This time, I purchased two books:

- *Thank God I'm Natural,* by Chris-Tia Donaldson
- *The Science of Natural Hair,* by Audrey Davis-Sivasothy

I got on YouTube and watched Naturals who were very popular at the time, mostly Taren Guy and Nikki Mae; they always kept my attention and were quite informative. Once I made up my mind that I was transitioning, I treated my relaxed hair as if it were already natural. This time was going to be different because I was different. I didn't just want to return to my natural hair; I was making a life decision to stop treating my hair as my attention magnet. But putting this lesson into practice was easier said than done.

During my six-month transition, I wore my hair styled with curlformers; a tool used to coil the hair into a spiral, great for managing two textures.

**Visit www.sisterswithbeauty.com/curlformers
to see me apply Curlformers.**

I switched to Senegalese twists to get me through the last three months of my transition. During these times, it was really hard because I kept getting anxious to see what I looked like when I wasn't trying to get people to see my hair instead of me. Watching all of the YouTube natural hairstyle videos only made me want to see my own hair texture that much more. Imagine that. After cutting, coloring, relaxing, and weaving my hair for half of my life, I was excited to see what it really looked like.

On Nov 27, 2010, at approximately 11:00 a.m., in San Antonio, Texas, I trusted a hairstylist to complete my Big Chop (or Butterfly Chop, as I like to call it). The experience felt so right. I could feel the weight of being the person always making changes to herself lifted off of me almost instantly. Any changes from here on out would be about me wanting to discover myself for who I truly was.

**Visit www.sisterswithbeauty.com/butterfly-chop
to watch my Butterfly Chop video.**

I followed a plan, one that I set for myself based on my lifestyle and my hair needs. I opted for a super-short cut because I didn't want to miss my transformation, which I felt was long overdue. I wanted to do the work, and I needed to learn who I really was without any smoke and mirrors to hide behind. I didn't want to chemically treat my hair at all, so I decided I wouldn't color my natural hair, as I had done while being relaxed. I wouldn't straighten my natural hair, as my hair had been straight for over twenty-four years of my life. I would just style it and be on my way. It was time for my hair to finally get a say in how I cared for it. I got so in tune with my hair and all of the things I was learning about natural hair that I started SistersWithBeauty (www.sisterswithbeauty.com). I wanted to empower others to know they could still be fly with natural hair.

One of the ways I did this was by creating a beauty series to help women understand their own beauty and how they could apply it to their everyday lives.

Visit www.sisterswithbeauty.com/beauty-videos
to become a part of the Butterfly Transition community
and enjoy the beauty videos and other perks.

Having shorter hair made me face myself because there was nothing to hide behind. For the first time ever, I felt like people could see me and not my representative. But my hair didn't stay short for long. As I gained a few inches, I reverted back to my childhood experience with hair length.

If my hair wasn't going to be long, it was indeed going to be styled to perfection.

"We can all return to our natural hair, but no two transitions are the same."

—DIANA RAMSEY

# 2 | Welcome to My Transition

When I returned to my natural hair the second time, I was prepared. The first thing I did was envision what my natural hair would look like. I daydreamed about my hair texture, afro, hair length, and everything down to my first puff ponytail. I had figured it all out. What I would look like natural was all I could think about. It never dawned on me that the woman in my vision wasn't real, or better put, she was a fantasy.

One day, while playing with the back of my hair during my six-month transition, I decided to do a small cut to discover what my hair would feel like, curl like, look like. So I cut and wet the back of my hair while still wearing Senegalese twists as my transition style. My hair didn't quite look or feel as I expected. I didn't understand it at the time, but looking back on that moment, I was in denial and afraid to admit this natural hair thing was like jumping out a window.

I really didn't know what to expect. Sure, I'd seen the excitement of others loving their hair, or better yet, giving the impression of loving it, but I wasn't impressed by my first introduction to my natural hair. I didn't have one clue as to what I would look like, or for that matter, if I would even like it. What I did know was that the person I had envisioned I would be after I was completely natural might never reveal herself to me.

This #FantasyNatural, the person I pictured I would be, the woman whose texture, length, and manageability I knew, this was the person I had believed I would be in the end.

My #FantasyNatural encouraged me the most during the initial months of my transition. However, she didn't show up during my Big Chop. She was too close to perfection. But this didn't stop me from daydreaming about what my hair would look like and feel like. It didn't stop my growth aspirations. My #FantasyNatural didn't help me embrace my journey any more than a thief can help you find stolen money.

It took me over three months after my haircut to get this vision of what my hair should look like out of my head. The ideas of what I wanted my hair to be, how long I wanted it to grow, and the type of texture I hoped to have all had to disappear.

I had to delete what I wanted from my hair so that I could continue my journey with realistic expectations. But it wasn't easy. There were times I didn't know I had a #FantasyNatural embedded in my journey, but countless length checks, comparing my hair to others, and disappointments showed me how much I did. I had to say goodbye to my idea of the #FantasyNatural. My natural hair was just that, my natural hair. Had I written down what I thought I would have during the early part of my journey, I would have been able to go back to those thoughts and appreciate my journey even more.

My transition journey wouldn't be perfect any more than I would see my imperfections made perfect over that time. This one lesson would take the span of five years to understand and still is a work in progress today.

Returning to my natural hair was going to require me to be open minded about who I was to become. I couldn't wish myself into another hair texture, length, or thickness any more than I could wish myself into another life. This transition was going to be a battle. I had to stop wanting what others thought was beautiful and learn to love me as my own beautiful.

Transitions can be so demanding and uncomfortable. I've heard other women talk about their #FantasyNatural, and I've known many transitioning women who opted to stop because their hair didn't match their expectations. I didn't want to be one of them.

I kept asking myself, "How could my hair and life be in need of so much of my attention?"

## Hair Transition Exercise #1:
## Step Into Your Transition

Answer these questions to help you step into your hair transition.

1. How does your hair make you feel today?

_____

_____

2. Why do you want to return back to your natural hair?

_____

_____

3. What type of natural hair texture would you like to have?

_____

_____

4. How long do you want your natural hair to grow? (Neck, shoulder, mid-back, I want to sit on it.)

_____

_____

"You can't miss what you've never had, but you will always dream about what could have been."

—DIANA RAMSEY

# 3 | Hi Daddy, Bye Daddy

There was a time when I thought my brother was the most selfish person in the world. I resented him so much as a teen that these feelings stayed with me well into my adult years. As I write this, it has only been six years since I stopped blaming him for the absence of my father.

Within a month of returning to my natural hair and going through with the Big Chop, something started to nudge at me.

"Look for your father," the small voice said.

There I was, sitting in my truth in my new home in Texas, when I heard a faint voice that I had never heard before. I knew my move to Texas was going to push me outside of my comfort zone, but looking for my biological father seemed a bit too much and rather complicated. I had spent so many years not hearing the voice call out to me that I never noticed it had been speaking all along.

I was not conceived from a loving marriage with two parents happily awaiting my arrival. Although my parents were friends, I know from my mother's account, they were just friends and in no way trying to be tied together for life with a child. My biological father's name is Ronnie E. Pigram, a Chicago native.

He made his living as an entrepreneur. (Guess that's where I get it from.) He owned a car upholstery company and was really talented.

I grew up wanting the kind of dad Bill Cosby played on TV. Heathcliff Huxtable adored his family, always provided for them, and never left them unless he was sneaking out to get a hoagie or deliver a baby. On the other hand, my biological father was the dad over the phone because we lived more than a thousand miles apart, he in Illinois and I in California. I also maintained a relationship with my half-brother, who was my older brother by two years. He lived with my father and made sure he talked to me every chance he could when my dad called.

I didn't officially meet my father until I was eleven years old. My family escaped the dangers of gang violence and a racial divide brewing in California, all leading up to the OJ Simpson trial and the LA riots. We settled in Virginia and were finally close enough to visit my father, but it was me who would take the first steps to making the reunion happen. My Uncle George decided he was going to take a trip to Chicago to visit my grandfather and bring me along to finally meet my father. Surprisingly, my mother wasn't against this reunion and let me go with my bags packed and no pep talk on either who my father was as a person or who she knew him to be. My mother didn't speak about my father, good, bad, or indifferent. It was just a conversation that never happened; she never openly talked about him, and I never pushed to know more.

I remember wearing a black-and-white polka dot skirt with a white shirt and some sneakers to meet my father. My uncle dropped me off with the daddy I only knew over the phone. I knew him by voice, so when he said, "Hello, Diana," chills ran down my spine and into my heart. But I refrained from running into his arms and holding him tight. I guess interactions like that only happened when fathers actually knew their daughters.

My brother and I fell right into our big brother and little sister roles. He pushed me around and told me what to do, and I played with him and his friends all day. My moments with my father during the Chicago trip were brief, a bit emotionless on his part, and to the point. He gave me $150 for school clothes; I had never held so many twenty, ten, and five dollar bills in my life.

Upon my return home, my mother and I didn't talk much about my trip to meet my dad. All my life, my mother had been my father, so meeting him wasn't something I felt comfortable showing excitement over. In a way, I felt like it would have been a sign of betrayal to be so "Team Dad" when he didn't take one step towards seeing me himself. But to be honest, I did feel special when I was around him. I'd finally met the dad from over the phone; he *did* exist.

A year later, one hot summer day, the phone rang, and my mother was told the story of my big brother committing suicide after an argument he had with my father. The police were called. I guess my father knew my brother shouldn't be left alone with his guns in the house, but before my father could convince the police to remove his firearms, a single shot went off.

My big brother was gone; he was fourteen years old.

My mother broke the news to me, and I sat stuck in that moment for years. I spent weeks at my best friend's house, escaping the emotional effects of death. Had I known I'd not only lose a brother but a father too, I would have begged my uncle to make one more trip back to Chicago, just to show my Dad he still had one child left among the living. After this horrific moment in time, my father disappeared from my life, but more importantly, from the world. I never spoke to him again. Inside I was crying, "I'm still alive. Love me. Be my Dad!"

Calls went unanswered until the phone line was disconnected. I lost touch with the part of me that was always a mystery. I'd never seen a woman on my father's side; any questions I ever had about him or his family would go unanswered. I had been cut off from a world I'd only started to want to know more about.

From that moment, I hardened myself to everything and everyone, especially men. My feelings about my father's absence bled into my core and made me internalize his absence. I wondered what was it about me that made him not want to stay. I hadn't committed suicide; I was still waiting for him to be my dad.

I found many ways to suppress the longing to have my father in my life. Over the years, a range of emotions flooded my mind, sadness, loneliness, and then finally, anger. I decided I would become successful. Yes, now that was a good idea. I would make him wish he had stayed in my life when I made it big and was sitting on Oprah's couch, talking about how his absence made me stronger. But what would success do? All I wanted was a father to talk to, run to, and inevitably, love me. How could I tell my mother I missed what I never ever truly had? So I didn't. I remained silent and grew up trying to fill the void of wanting the one person too far from my understanding to hold on to.

I became self-sufficient at twelve years old. I learned how to not need anything from anyone because they were always liable to leave me. My independence was ignited by the disappearing acts of my father.

It took me well into my thirties to admit I was a black girl with daddy issues. Relationships with men were influenced by the idea that they could pick up without a trace and leave me. The crazy thing is I ran into a few who actually did.

As the small voice encouraged me to look for my father, I set the wheels in motion to do just that, but discouragement stopped me from continuing my search. I didn't know much about him or other family members to help fill in the holes. I became discouraged, ashamed, and angry about having to look for him in the first place. Then one day, I just stopped.

I called off the search, stopped looking, and told myself if he didn't care, then neither did I.

I didn't need him.

I didn't need anyone.

"Where there are no lessons, there is no growth."

—DIANA RAMSEY

# 4 | My Transition Plan

A wise man once said, "If you fail to plan, then you plan to fail." Because I had lived this quote during my initial hair transition and failure, I knew the second time had to be different. Instead of doing the same thing and expecting a different result, I changed how I went about transitioning the second time. I decided I would create a transition plan. This plan would identify how long I would maintain my relaxed and natural hair, the date I would officially do the Big Chop, and even the styles I would wear until I completed my process. If I wanted to be successful in my hair transition, I needed to do something to show I was serious. Creating my transition plan was just the kind of idea I needed to keep me on the right path.

In talking to Naturals who are currently transitioning, I always ask them what their plan is. Normally my question is met with a series of blank stares and unfilled silence, and then a few ummms seal the deal. This all means many of them don't have a transition plan, and I can understand what that looks like because I too started my hair transition without a transition plan. But I failed at that attempt because I failed to plan.

I felt helpless as my hair continued to knot up due to being dehydrated. I wasn't using products that could live up to my hair's new demands. My shampoo was basically full-blown sulfate from the sulfate tree (seriously). My conditioner didn't have any properties to properly coat my hair or help retain moisture.

I've noticed that many people who return to their natural hair (including me) start off with no plan. For the most part, they have an idea, but they are uncertain as to how they will execute it. There is no vision, and where there is no vision there can be little hope. There was a time when I believed it was okay to not have a transition plan, but now planning is one of my best insights on how to carry out a successful hair transition.

When I began maintaining both my relaxed and natural hair, it was important to understand what the line of demarcation (LOD) meant. The LOD is the point where your natural and relaxed hair meet. This line is special, fragile, and significant, and it was important to pay attention to it when I managed my hair.

I sat down to evaluate the type of transition plan I was going to implement and realized early on there were going to be a few options to choose from. I mapped out three types of transition plans and still advocate their usage today.

## Plan A: Short Term (0 to 3 months)

If I wanted to get my transition over with, this plan would have been perfect for me.

Short-term plans are just that, plans carried out for a short time frame of zero to three months. The short-term transition would have given me a short window of opportunity to educate myself. Ensuring I was educated on all things natural was very important to me because I had failed at doing so the first time around. I didn't want to skip or miss information, so I knew planning to cut too soon wasn't in my cards. But maybe this option is for you.

A short-term transition is followed by a short cut, such as rocking a Caesar or Teeny Weeny Afro (TWA), and doing it all in under three months' time. When you carry out this plan, you're able to see your new growth to the fullest extent. You're meeting yourself all over again. All plans come with frustration in trying to decide which products, regimen, and treatments work for your hair. But I like to believe the discovery is the best part about Plan A, B, or C.

Plan A will test many things you never knew about yourself, while highlighting the best parts about you.

## Plan B: Midterm (4 to 11 months)

This was the transition plan for me. I knew I wanted to grow a little more of my natural hair before my Big Chop.

If you choose this plan, you're possibly like me, wanting just a little more of your natural hair to grow before officially jumping out there all the way. I chose this plan because it allowed me to grow a little, both in my hair and my confidence, and it allowed me to test a few products on my hair while I was in transition. You'll spend time growing a few more inches of natural hair before officially making the cut (Big Chop). During this time, the frustration of managing two textures can get high, so high you may cut a little sooner than your initial date. Discovery is still a part of this plan. Sure you'll possibly have more hair to play with, but you still get to experience all of the newness your hair has to offer.

## Plan C: Long Term (1 year or more)

I know one thing about those who choose to transition for one or more years; they are the most patient people.

I knew early on, once I'd established the transition plans that this one was not for me. I was far too nosy, anxious, and impatient. But that's not everyone; some women are able to sit comfortably and grow their hair out. If you choose this plan, you are very patient and will possibly have seven or more inches of natural hair once you officially cut off your relaxed ends. You'll also have to master styling two textures, which can be difficult and stressful at times. Many who choose this path find they are a bit unaware of how to deal with their natural hair once they cut off the relaxed ends. If you opt for a longer transition, you won't have a year or more of experience managing just your natural hair. However, your hair will have grown a bit longer, and in my understanding, this is why some naturals opt for the long-term transition in the first place.

I realized no matter which plan I chose I was going to be faced with challenges I had to overcome. During my short-term transition, I fought insecurities about my "Steve Harvey" fro. I questioned if my hair was truly growing or if I would always look like the reflection looking back at me in the mirror. Although my decision to transition was solid, I had fears, insecurities, and questions that only I could answer. None of these things stopped me from moving forward, but they did rest heavily on my shoulders. In the midst of it all, I was the face of my brand and of my new lifestyle. Many times, I pushed my own needs to the side to ensure I posted a style video, treatment regimen, or update on my hair. During these times, I avoided my own life while trying to breathe life into my business. SistersWithBeauty was growing, and my life was going to have to take a number and get in line.

My best tip for anyone trying to figure out her transition plan is to open your calendar and mark the date you believe you want to be officially natural. This date is the day you stop living in between relaxed and natural and truly go the distance in your discovery. This one action gave me a sense of accountability with a clear starting point to my hair transition.

You can't start anything if you don't know where you are going or when you plan to get there. Crafting my transition plan helped me get there on time and better prepared.

## Hair Transition Exercise #2:
## Transition Plan Contract

*This is your contract between you and your tresses. Sign your name below and remember a contract is only as good as the people willing to uphold the agreement.*

I will carry out my transition plan and officially return to my natural hair on _____(mm/dd/yyyy).

Signature: _____

Date: _____

"There is no greater division than not being able to make a decision."

—DIANA RAMSEY

# 5 | Styling Two Textures

I never realized styling two textures would be like babysitting two kids with totally different upbringings and personalities. The amount of time I chose to work with my two textures (natural + relaxed) was short lived. I decided early on that my hair transition was not going to be one in which I spent more than six months trying to transition. I didn't want to maintain two textures for too long, out of fear that I would chicken out of the process all together. I had seen it happen too many times before and didn't want to be the next on the list.

In the beginning, styling both my relaxed and natural hair wasn't so bad. I opted for flexi rod and curlformer styles. These styles acted as a great concealer of the two textures in constant battle for my attention. The day I decided to choose a transition plan was the same day I stopped wondering how long I was going to have to referee my hair into submission. To keep myself on track, I started writing my official transition date down everywhere I could. Go ahead and put your date here, just in case you haven't written it down yet: _____. This date is what I like to call your #NatDay; this was also the day things got real when it came to my hair transition. I was no longer trying out a return to natural. After this date, I would be officially natural with more work to do on the back-end than before. Up until that point, I had been standing between two textures and two lifestyles, it was exhausting.

The stress of dealing with both textures, while trying to understand all of the rules or guidelines for natural hair, was almost too much to bear. You are not the only one doing wall slides to the floor in your bathroom because I, too, was a slider. Sometimes I even opted to slide in the shower, trying to drown in my own hopelessness, but I digress. It was difficult styling two textures, but after a while I started to track how I could make it better on myself. Taking notes along the way to encourage me and show me how far I had come was helpful.

The first thing I realized was that I needed to stop trying to do the most with my transitioning hair; too many styles and changes led to early breakage and higher frustrations. Once I tried a low-manipulation approach, by adding Senegalese twists during my transition, life as I knew it changed. I then planned styles I would do one after the other to lessen my concern about figuring out what to do next with my hair.

I rotated five styles into my routine and kept them as my go-to styles during my transition. By putting these five styles into rotation, I spent more time enjoying my journey than being frustrated by it.

Your two textures are not the same. They are perfect strangers being made to live together for a brief moment in time. I'm not going to say they don't like one another; there is just a major difference between the two. They will never look the same, act the same, respond the same, nor be the same. It's like East Coast versus West Coast gang wars.

Here are my five go to styles that assisted me all the way to the end of my transition.

## Bantu Knot Out

There are many reasons why I love a Bantu knot out. It often gave me a wavy spiral that I haven't been able to duplicate with any other style. Keep in mind that no two Bantu knot outs are ever the same. This style always met me with a surprise because it never looked the same the next time I tried to style my hair.

## Braid Out/Twist Out

My two favorite styles. If you're going to do a braid out or twist out, I suggest putting rollers at the ends of your hair to enhance your texture throughout the style. The last thing you want is straight ends. I always wanted to be considerate to my relaxed ends. They were straight due to the chemical compounds I'd applied; I kept this in mind when styling both textures.

## Flat-Twist Ponytail

Flat-twisting my hair and adding a ponytail extension or simply tucking my relaxed ends into a ball was the lifeline to my natural hair getting a break from my relaxed hair. I've rocked this style many ways and continued to do this style well past my five-year mark. It's easy on your morning routine and light on the manipulation side as well. It's also a great style to workout in.

## Hat-Scarf Combo

This little number was crafted by the need to go to the store and my weird desire to always layer everything. There I was with my scarf wrapped around my head, but something was missing, so I grabbed my hat and bam! The hat-scarf combo was born. During the weekends, I spend more time moving my fingers on the computer keys than styling my hair. This style is a way to show my creative side while forcing myself to take a hair break. I can't style what I can't see. Wearing a hat and a scarf might not be your thing, and I'm cool with that. Choose one or the other, but remember you could very well do both and be okay.

# Flexi Rod Set

Flexi rod sets are the easiest way to wear both textures out during your transition. During the creation of this style, both textures are beaten into a super-coiled spiral state. What I like about this style is that, no matter your texture, it forces your hair into submission. It's like telling two fighting kids to play nice or else bad things will happen.

These five styles allowed me to successfully wear both textures without noticing the line of demarcation or applying additional stress. They are the most sought-after styling options in the natural hair community. Using and learning them during your transition will help in your overall styling options for today and in the future.

Take one more look at the list and decide which style you will attempt first. If you want to see these styles in different variations, visit the link below and check out the special page created just for you.

- Bantu knot out
- Braid out/Twist out
- Flat-twist ponytail
- Hat-scarf combo
- Flexi rod set

Visit www.sisterswithbeauty.com/transition-styles
to see my 5 Transition Styles.

## Hair Transition Exercise #3:
## Transition Styles Plan

Which style do you think you want to try immediately? Write it down, and take a picture when you wear the style. Use #ButterflyTransition and share your picture on Twitter and Instagram so we can all celebrate with you.

Style: _____

Date: _____

"Blind are the people who wish for others to see things the same way."

—DIANA RAMSEY

# 6 | Natural with No Fanfare

I did it. My hair was natural, and now the real work on myself could begin.

I remember reading horrific stories about Naturals' first day back at work after the Big (Butterfly) Chop. Still, I had decided I was going to cut off all of my relaxed hair on November 27, 2010, which was a Saturday. I told no one at work and kept it all to myself, thinking I would rearrange their mindset come the following Monday.

In my mind, it was about to be the March on Washington after my chop, and I was going to blow everyone away with my strength, confidence, and amazing haircut. I had watched too many YouTube videos and read too many blog posts about other women's experiences and their newfound sense of self once they big-chopped. It was as if every Butterfly who did the Big Chop received her "I'm Blacker" card in the mail immediately. Like she instantly knew more, moved better, and inevitably could take on anything or anyone because she was strong, like her hair. Upon entering my office, I braced myself for hard criticisms, mean looks, disappointment, and my own bit of canned adversity because that's what I thought would happen.

What I got was silence.

Let me explain. I received not one ounce of acknowledgment, attention, side eye, second glances, or words of any kind about my new look.

Nothing. It was a ghost town.

My co-workers carried on about their day as usual, and I was dumbfounded. I had cut my hair with no fanfare, no celebration, no questions, or racist attitudes. I mean for God's sake, I was in Texas, and no one was acting as expected or showing out. I had prepared myself to not be surprised if someone said something slick out the side of their neck, but lack of response made me feel crazy.

After spending an entire day being ignored for my "say it loud, I'm Black and I'm proud" baby fro, I began to question myself. Did I do this for me or for them? And exactly what did I expect as a response to a personal life decision? This was about my life as much as it was about my hair, and on a life note, in hindsight, my growth not being recognized by others was a good thing. It meant no outside influencers could persuade me from being myself, but in that moment I didn't see it that way. I was giving my power away because I wanted others to care enough to react. I didn't want to admit the fear of cutting my hair was still dwelling within me. I wanted their opposition to confirm I had made a good decision. I welcomed the friction, and when I didn't get it, I was left with my own decision, alone.

It's funny how you can plan out so many of your hair choices without understanding it's really your life you are changing. In order to change my hair, I too had to make a change and stop giving other people my power through my hair. The memories of what others thought came back into my mind; I still needed to hear the admiration, and I still wanted the praise that I had done something right. This moment in my natural existence only uncovered that I was still in need of compliments. I was still placing the responsibility of acceptance on my hair.

The entire day went by, and just as I thought no one was going to make a comment, my co-worker parted his lips at the end of our meeting and said, "Oh, by the way, nice cut."

I'm not invisible in this place? You *do* see me?

I would love to sit here and tell you I didn't care what others thought, and that, at that moment, I had taken back my power to accept my own look, but I hadn't. I was thousands of miles away from my family and friends, and I felt ignored. Like if I shouted in a room full of people no one would hear me. The feeling of being ignored and invisible was an uncomfortable feeling to me. I had used my hair as a conversation piece for so long while relaxed I thought surely I knew how to get people's attention. When I didn't get the expected response, I began to doubt my new life and my new hair.

I cared, and yes, it mattered that my response wasn't even a coin toss in the direction of disrupting the day. I spent most of the day being in my feelings over the perceived lack of interest in my hair and life transition. Meanwhile, I was mentally trying to lift myself up by singing, "I am not my hair," knowing in that moment I was lying to myself.

In that moment, I was my hair, because I wanted people to see me through it, and there was no disassociating from that fact. I wanted someone to pay attention to me that day, to recognize something different was happening in-side of me, to pinch me to see if I was real, but that pinch never came. It would take five years for me to realize that pinch of my own realness and authenticity would have to come from me. To admit that I wasn't there yet was far too scary, so I didn't. I avoided the calling to grow in that moment.

My hair transition gave me a simple, superficial way to see my own beau-ty. However, my life transition was nagging at me to be honest; my avoidance only prolonged my lessons, growth, and purpose. I had hidden my needs so deep I didn't even realize what I was lacking or in need of. The early stages of my hair transition only scratched the surface of what I had been hiding from myself all my life.

"When you spread your wings, you give yourself permission to share your beauty with the world."

—DIANA RAMSEY

# 7 | Learning Natural Hair Tools & Basics

Before I washed, styled, or attempted to maintain my hair, I should have sat down and mapped out all the hair tools I would need. In the beginning, I was still trying to part my hair and brush it with the same tools from my relaxed days. This is the mistake most of us make in our transition. At first, I didn't see what the problem was. Why not use the same tools on my natural hair too? Well, what seems like a simple answer now wasn't so simple then. I assumed it was all just hair, my hair, and I could use the same tools with little to no problem. But my natural hair wasn't the same. Matter of fact, it was foreign to me, so my assumption, although logical, was wrong.

My natural hair required special attention, special combs and brushes, clips and holders to ensure the tools I used were not responsible for taking my hair out or damaging it in any way. After throwing away every tool I'd owned when I was relaxed, I switched everything up and wrote this inventory list of tools every natural needs to survive during her hair transition.

- Wide-tooth comb
- Wide-tooth brush
- Rattail comb
- Butterfly clips
- Bonnet
- Hair drain catcher (bonus tool)

I needed the **wide-tooth comb** to detangle, and it became my saving grace, as my hair grew longer. Prior to maintaining my natural hair, it hadn't been difficult to get a comb through my hair. But that all changed once I put down the relaxer and traded my touch-up for a Big Chop. I don't think people talked about the complexities of detangling and combing through your natural hair as much during the time I transitioned. It took me over three years to perfect my detangle regimen, but I finally got it down to a five-minute science. One of my biggest errors was using the wrong hair tool to complete the detangling process.

Over the years, I tested ways to detangle best and settled on using only one tool for the job. I would use a wide-tooth comb or a **wide-tooth brush**. I found I lost more hair when I used both a wide-tooth comb and brush at the same time, so I chose to only use one. Opting to use both only took more of my hair out and added unnecessary stress to my hair. The wide-tooth comb allowed my hair to pass through without snagging on every single curl, coil, and kink.

The next tool that stole my heart was my **rattail comb**. I didn't realize its importance until I parted my hair for the first time with this tool. My hair separated like the Red Sea and obeyed the comb's commands. The rattail comb with the metal end specialized in precision parting and became my new best friend. I used a rattail comb, more specifically a pintail comb, for parting my hair as it got longer.

**Butterfly clips** were another great asset in my natural tool chest. During parting, using butterfly clips helped to keep my hair out of the way and allowed me to style with no interruption. I built quite a collection of these clips, and I still faithfully use them to this day during washing and styling.

But none of these tools could compare to my **bonnet**. My silk bonnet held me down and kept my hair moisturized. Cotton scarves and wraps absorb too much of your hair's moisture to be protective and safe. I knew I wasn't interested in buying a satin pillow case, yet I own more than twenty bonnets. They are inexpensive, and once you get a good inventory, you'll see how amazing it is to have more than just one.

By the time I had celebrated my first year natural, I realized I had washed my hair more in one year than I had ever washed my hair when I was relaxed. But there was a negative effect from all that hair washing in the shower. My drains became backed up and ended up being very expensive to get professionally cleaned out. As a precaution, my last tool I added to the list was a **hair drain catcher**. I had gotten too excited washing my hair in the shower. Although movies showed other races enjoying this activity every day, it wasn't the case in my life. I still know women who have never washed their hair in the shower. Having a drain catcher cut down on my plumbing costs immediately. I also added a sink snake to clean out some of those hairs that got past the hair drain catcher.

I wasn't playing games with my hair anymore. Changes were being made every day to keep up with my hair's needs. If I had to stop using or start using a tool to keep my hair healthy, that was exactly what I did. But having new tools without understanding natural hair basics was like having the keys to a new car and not remembering where you parked. It was pointless to have all of the best tools and not know how to use them. I became focused and determined to learn how to care for my hair better. Sure there was YouTube, but no one knew my hair, not even me, so it was time to become more acquainted with my tresses, and the lessons began with washing.

## #1. Regular washing is a must.

I had to throw away the old motto "Dirty hair is healthy." I can't begin to understand where this came from, but for a time or two, I believed it during my relaxed days and washed my hair less. But that wasn't the case with my natural hair. Dirt did hurt, and I had to banish this idea completely while incorporating thick butters and styling creams to perfect my hairstyles. The quality of my hair relied on it being clean and moisturized. I spent more than two years studying different hair-washing techniques and regimens. Every week, I washed my hair and tweaked or changed how many steps I included. All this testing resulted in me releasing the SWB 10-Step Wash Day Regimen. I wanted the same results, if not better, every time I washed my hair. I wanted to know all of my work was going to cleanse, restore, and balance my hair during every wash. I achieved that every time with the SWB 10-Step Wash Day Regimen.

Visit www.sisterswithbeauty.com/wash-day to get your free download of the SWB 10-Step Wash Day Regimen.

## #2. Moisture isn't a product; it's an action.

I had a small stint of time during which I was a product junkie. I was buying this product and that product after every new YouTube video I watched. It happened so much that I realized I didn't want to add to anyone else's product-junkie ways when I began doing style videos on the SistersWithBeauty YouTube Channel. I was searching for moisture in a product, not realizing that moisture wasn't a product. It wasn't something I could slather on my hair and call it well balanced. If I wanted moisture, I was going to have to work to get it. That's when I learned moisturizing my hair was a process and not a product. There was actually no product on the market that could give me moisture. It became very important to properly cleanse my hair with shampoo and balance with conditioners that were able to close my hair follicle and assist with moisture retention. Wash my hair regularly, drink water, steam, hot oil, and deep conditioner treatments. Taking these actions helped add moisture back into my hair.

## #3. Out with the sulfate.

I kept hearing about this sulfate ingredient being bad, and I had already had my run-in with sulfate and what it could do during my first attempt at returning to my natural hair. Remember my matted hair-washing experience? Well, that was due to me using a shampoo with a high percentage of sulfates in it, as it was a clarifying shampoo. Sulfate is one of the many ingredients that is not here for my natural hair or yours, but it's found in many of your current shampoo bottles. Don't believe me? Go under your sink and check. It is a harsh cleansing agent that is used to produce suds, but it does more damage than good. It does more than just remove product build-up; it can dull your colored tresses, damage your hair follicles, and promote breakage.

Once I learned about sulfate, I acted like it was a creditor, and we don't answer their phone calls where I'm from. I became aware of which companies were using sulfate in their products and which weren't. Other ingredients were added to my watch list, but the main culprits, sulfate or sodium laureth sulfate, each do the same thing, strip hair of its natural oils.

## #4. Water is good.

I figured out the best way to hydrate and provide moisture to the largest organ in my body (skin) is by drinking water. Increasing my water intake wasn't easy because I had to first admit to not drinking enough water. Then I had to educate myself and even ask my doctor what was the appropriate amount of water I needed to consume for my body to be hydrated. Your skin needs water for hydration and contrary to the "dirt don't hurt" theory, my hair also loved water. I began to drink more water and became religious about washing my hair every week. I couldn't rely on Google to help me determine how much water I should consume, so I went to my doctor. I mean that's why I pay for insurance, right? My doctor was able to recommend my water consumption based on my age, height, weight, and lifestyle. Your doctor will be able to base your consumption on all of these criteria and sort out any uncertainty you have after asking Google.com.

## #5. Protect your ends.

I didn't initially realize that my ends needed protection until they began to show signs of distress. During my transition and even after my Big Chop, understanding the importance of well-managed, protected ends went a long way in how my styles looked. The overall quality of my hair depended on how much love and TLC I gave my ends. It was my job to tame, tuck, and protect them.

## #6. Practice a Night Natural Regimen. #NNR

I prepared my hair at night for the hair I wanted to have in the morning. I did this by developing a night-time regimen to be carried out consistently, even when I was dog-dead sleepy.

Yes, I am admitting to styling my hair every night so that I don't have to do it in the morning. I very rarely wake up and do a massive style in the morning. Outside of removing my two-strand or flat twists, I'm out the door in less that fifteen minutes. Here is what my night-regimen steps look like:

1.  Apply a light mist of water.
2.  Apply styling cream or butter.
3.  Run my handheld steamer through medium to large sections of my hair to add moisture back into the follicle.
4.  Twist and/or style my hair at night.

You thought I was going to say something more, didn't you?
My nighttime regimen is very simple; I restore my moisture balance and

get out of there. Twisting my hair has been my saving grace, and styling at night gave me back more time in the morning.

I became a true believer in the "work smarter and never harder" concept. I dedicated a lot of time to learning my natural hair basics. It was almost as if I was back in school, picking up a new trade.

# Hair Transition Exercise #4:
## Applying Your Natural Basics.

Set a date when you will start incorporating each one of the 5 Natural Hair Basics into your journey. This is all about accountability. Choose a date, and fill in the sections with that date.

1. I will incorporate regular washing on: _____
2. I will incorporate a moisture action on: _____
3. I will remove all sulfate products on: _____
4. I will increase my water intake on: _____
5. I will start to protect my ends on: _____

"What others think
can't be more important
than what you know."

—DIANA RAMSEY

# 8 | That Hair Won't Get You Where You Want to Be

I had taken a job in DC by the time I was four years into my natural hair journey. As I sat in a project meeting with my fro sitting high and my expertise raining all over the meeting, I felt like I was on top of the world. I had relocated back to DC from Texas and was currently running the team meeting at my new job like a boss.

I was on fire, shooting back questions and laying down my own two cents. As the meeting concluded, I was pulled to the side by a respected individual in the office and told:

*"That hair won't get you where I know you want to be."*

I was frozen. My heart stopped, and all the blood rushed from my brain to my feet because my mind was blown. As my body internally rejected what was happening, I couldn't help but wonder why hadn't I appreciated the silence about my hair in Texas? There, I showed up to work after my Big Chop to silence, but here, in DC, my hair was always the topic of discussion. If I changed my hair, the questions were about how long the style took. Why had I never tried to be a hairdresser? And how did my hair go from big to curly to short all in one day? They were all so fascinated and perplexed at the same time.

However, this statement offended me—period.

As I continued to engage in conversation with this person, I realized this was my moment. The opposition, the adversity, it seemed a little late since I had been natural for four years, but hey, it was here. I was told to come by for a mentoring session to discuss the topic of hair in the workplace. But the damage from the comment was already done. I felt like I was being judged and assessed, and to someone, on that day, my hair didn't match up to the success my career was on.

I went home and took to social media to blow off my frustration and tell someone who would understand what had been said to me at work. I didn't realize this action alone activated me to be the spokesperson for the "What are you going to do next, girl?" conversation. I welcomed debate about my hair, myself, and my actions leading up to my meeting.

Two months passed before my mentoring session, but the time leading up to the session was met with my strong sense of self, stronger than I had ever felt before about my hair. I proclaimed I would wear my hair the same all the way until the time I met with the person, and I did. I even titled the event #FroGate.

**FroGate**: noun. The moment when someone judges you based on your natural hair and their assumptions of how it should look.

I wore my fro loud, high, and in your face. I felt like my lifestyle was being challenged, I was being asked to tone it down or at least to look differently when coming into my place of work. As I sat across the table discussing the statement and how it offended me, I realized we were from two different times.

*"That hair won't get you where I know you want to be."*

I'm sure during the time that this older woman was launching and maneuvering her own career, this message was communicated to her. I've seen other women of color play small when we were the giants in the room. We've straightened up our acts and ironed out the kinks in our differences, just to be seen as equal. This is what I came to understand when talking to the woman who, two months earlier, offended me by her negative comments about my hair.

I wasn't there to convince her, and she wasn't there to persuade me. We continued our conversation and came to an understanding that good intent but poor word choice led to much of our misunderstanding.

I know there are many horror stories about people being judged for wearing their natural hair at work. Through my experience in this particular situation, I learned how to have open dialogue, not to just be heard, but to listen intently to why people feel the way they do. Neither of us could change our age nor our perceptions that were influential by our life experiences. But on that day, I fell in love with my hair in a different way. I was super protective and not because I wanted someone to admire my hair, but because I stood on the other side of admiration and still loved myself. On that day, I left my office feeling the most empowered about my hair and how much it was changing me.

"We give fear a name, a personality, and the power to continuously hold us back."

—DIANA RAMSEY

# 9 | Fear of Flying: 365 Days of Fear

I didn't know I had a fear of flying until I sat on plans to release my jewelry line for 365 days. Although this wasn't the only fear I allowed to derail me, it was the fear that broke me. In discovering how long I allowed fear to reside in my life, I became even weaker in its grasp.

My breakdown came at a moment when I was no longer able to emotionally hold in what I had become afraid of. I had begun execution on two projects I thought were great ideas:

1. Butterfly Jewelry line
2. Bet It All on Black (BIAOB)

These two extensions of SistersWithBeauty were set to come out in the beginning of 2015. I had informed other business friends about BIAOB, and I set up a focus group for my Butterfly Jewelry line. I often daydreamed about people's responses to both of these ideas, but I never envisioned what would happen next.

I set up a focus group for the jewelry line with clientele from Nubian Hueman (www.NubianHueman.com), a fashion boutique in Washington, DC. I wanted to keep the secret of the release while I gathered feedback, and using SistersWithBeauty followers would have given away too much. I studied all of the things I would need for an official focus group and made sure every detail was executed to perfection.

According to focus group guidelines, the client is never to be in the room during the focus group. They are too invested in the product or idea to be able to handle direct feedback from others. I knew this and hadn't planned to be in the room the day of the focus group. However, my videographer had a death in the family the morning of the focus group, and I made the executive decision to film the event and go incognito so no one would recognize me.

This was my first mistake, but I really didn't have a choice.

"Are we being punked?"

"Is this really the jewelry line?"

"It looks like a twelve-year-old made this in her basement."

The feedback from the focus group was harsh, especially since I had to hear it live. I really shouldn't have been in the room to hear every aspect of what the group thought. I held myself together but the chains holding my emotions broke the second the last person from the group left with her parting gift.

I realized two of things during the focus group.

1.  I need to practice my emotional walk-out.

Mine was horrible and it got even sadder when the doorstopper wouldn't cooperate and jammed, keeping me from closing (slamming) the door behind me.

2.  I should have used SWB clientele.

I believe I would have gotten more useful feedback on the pieces from women who actually identified with the butterfly theme and concept.

The feedback hurt like 1000 knives stabbing me in my side. The pain cut so deeply that I went home and boxed up everything. All the jewelry got put in the darkest corner of my house and of my mind.

Unfortunately, I also boxed up Bet It All on Black. I didn't receive anything negative to keep me from moving forward with it, but it did get caught in the crossfire. All the work I had put into both of these projects stopped, and before I knew what was happening, a whole year passed before I saw either of them again.

I let fear win over my growth, my life, and my lessons. I acted unfazed; I created new projects, focused on other ideas, and thought I had done a great job simply moving on. My pride wasn't going to admit I let the focus group change my mind and my goals. It wasn't the attendees' fault they didn't like the jewelry, but it was my fault to think they would tell me they loved it when they didn't.

All my life I've had people approve of and like the things I did. One of the best things you can receive is constructive criticism, but when all you hear is "It's great; you always do a great job," you become stifled. This feedback, as raw as it felt, was foreign to me and hurt my feelings.

This moment was pulling me to grow and to expand, but in that moment, I didn't see it that way. I faced this time in my life with avoidance, an attitude, and a closed mind. Instead of growing up, I grew down and failed to release the Butterfly jewelry, Bet It All on Black, and anything else I was afraid of.

Fear, the thing that only exists if we say so, was living all around me. I had given fear a name, a place to stay, food, and even a warm bed to lie on, while I suffered the consequences of housing this horrible roommate. The first step to getting out of fear is being able to admit you're living in it.

Without discovering my fear, I probably would have never known I needed to get out of it.

"I can paint you a pretty picture; it's up to you to care what type of paint I am using."

—DIANA RAMSEY

# 10 | Product, Product, and Product—No Ingredients

When many Butterflies decide they want to return to their natural hair, they immediately ask, "What products should I use?" This question would make you believe that the most important thing about your natural hair journey is the products you use—and not the ingredients they are made of.

My interest in ingredients increased after my experience using sulfate shampoos. I knew the second time I transitioned that I needed to understand which ingredients to use and which to stay away from.

The ingredients label is the most exciting part of a product if you ask me. When I was done being romanced by a brand's idea of what their target audience looked like or wanted, I turned over the product bottle to read the label and identify ingredients. My first question was: "What is in this product that will allow it to do what it says it will do?" I wanted a solid product understanding.

Product understanding: noun. The process of learning to identify good and bad ingredients found in hair products.

As a consumer, I know it's my job to be smart about what I buy and, inevitably, why I buy it. I've been sold by effective marketing too, but as I became more aware, I wanted to know the ingredients of my products. The ingredients should captivate you and convince you to buy or try a product. When you look at your ingredients, the most potent within the mixture, are the ones listed first. However, this isn't always the case. If you find a product that has one of the ingredients listed below, check to see the placement of that ingredient to determine if it is prominent within the product. Once I had a better understanding of ingredients and how they enhanced a product or decreased its effectiveness, I drafted a list of a few ingredients I vowed to stay away from.

## Ingredients to Avoid

(List is not all encompassing.)

**Ammonium Lauryl Sulfate:** Strips hair and skin of their natural protective barriers, leaving you vulnerable to other potentially dangerous chemicals that may be in the products we use or in our environment.

**Diethanolamine (DEA):** Moderate cancer links, irritation to skin, eyes, or lungs.

**Isopropyl Alcohol:** Linked to headaches, flushing, dizziness, mental depression, nausea, vomiting, and coma. Commonly found in antifreeze, aftershave, and hair color rinses.

**Mineral Oil:** Linked to irritation of the skin, rash, hives, difficulty breathing, and tightness in the chest,  and swelling of the mouth, face, lips, and tongue. Commonly found in hair products, nail polishes, lip balm, skin lotions, and make-up remover.

**Monoethanolamine or Ethanolamine (MEA/ETA):** Linked to irritation of the skin, eyes, and lungs. Found mostly in hair coloring as a pH regulator. Used as an emulsifier.

**Parabens:** Linked to skin irritation and contact dermatitis. Commonly found in shampoos, toothpaste, and food additives.

**Petroleum:** Linked to breast tumors, suffocation of skin, premature aging, and aggravated acne. Commonly found in hair conditioners.

**Polyethylene Glycol (PEG):** Linked to immune system vulnerability and potentially carcinogenic (having the potential to cause cancer). Commonly found in cleaners, shampoos, and oven cleaners.

**Sodium Lauryl (Laureth) Sulfate:** Known to cause scalp irritation, tangled hair, swelling of the hands, face, and arms, and split and frizzy hair. Commonly found in shampoo, conditioner, and toothpaste.

**TEA Lauryl Sulfate:** Causes irritation, especially if allowed to contact the skin for significant periods of time.

**Triethanolamine (TEA/TEOA):** Increased tumors in the livers of mice. Strong evidence to suggest as a human immune and respiratory toxicant or allergen. Commonly found in shampoos, soaps, and facial cleaners.

It's important for us all to become aware of the ingredients used in our hair products. After compiling the list of bad ingredients, I became more aware of the amazing ingredients I found in my hair products. Although the below list isn't all encompassing, let me tell you, I live to find products using these ingredients.

## Good Ingredients to Look For
(List is not all encompassing.)

**Acyl-Coenzyme A Desaturase:** Protects the integrity of hair, preventing damage and breakage while enhancing curl definition.

**Aloe Barbadensis (Aloe Leaf Juice):** Found in moisturizer and humectant products as a main ingredient.

**Avocado Oil:** Moisturizes and strengthens hair strands, protecting hair from damage. A good source of vitamin E.

**Burdock Root:** Healing treatment of the skin and blood circulation.

**Butyrospermum Parkii (Shea oil):** Prevents hair breakage, stimulates healthy growth, and makes hair look shiny and healthy.

**D-Panthenol (Pro-Vitamin B5):** A humectant, emollient, and moisturizer. Helps to moisturize, shine, and add gloss.

**Jamaican Black Castor Seed Oil:** Hair softener, pre-poo deep conditioner, and scalp health nourisher.

**Jojoba Seed Oil:** Unclogs hair follicles to increase hair growth.

**Keratin Amino Acids:** Moisturize and keep hair shiny.

**Marshmallow Root Powder:** Provides an abundance of "slip," which helps to nourish and detangle.

**Organic Olea European (Olive Oil):** Restores moisture and nourishment to dry, rough skin and hair.

**Peppermint:** Scalp rinse for dry and itchy skin.

**Salicylic Acid:** Anti-dandruff agent. Opens clogged pores, neutralizes bacteria, and treats dandruff.

**Simmondsia Chinensis (Jojoba) Seed Oil:** Provides skin softness. Increased absorption into the pores and hair. Moisturizer and emollient.

**Sodium Lauryl Sulfoacetate:** Skin-friendly cleanser. Creates lather without stripping or irritating the skin.

**Stearic Acid:** Acts as a surfactant, removing dirt and sebum from hair. Gives condition to hair.

**Tiare Flower:** Improves hair texture and smooths hair follicles.

**Water:** It is vital and should be the first ingredient in all products you use for hydration of the hair and body. Drinking water also helps to hydrate your hair and body from the inside out. It eliminates hardness and strengthens your hair.

**Willow Bark Extract:** Enhances skin cell turnover by promoting exfoliation.

Visit www.sisterswithbeauty.com/category/ingredients-review to see a more in-depth view of three brands I've reviewed.

Here, I break down four of the most sought-after types of products:

- Shampoo
- Conditioner
- Deep Conditioner
- Styling Cream/Butter

Ingredients matter because I matter, you matter, our hair matters.

Visit www.sisterswithbeauty.com/favproducts
to see a list of My Favorite Products.

Your regimen will still be the most important thing in the entire process of using products, but don't get this one confused. Products matter when you're looking for something to yield a certain result. If you're using a product that doesn't have any ingredients that can get you there, trust me you need to know this, and fast. When evaluating a new product, do the following:

**Product Tip #1:** Use product as directed.
Don't make up your own usage rules when applying a product. If a product instructs you to leave it on no more than fifteen minutes, then set an alarm and try not to push too far past the required time. Sometimes it's not the product, but how the product is being applied that creates an unfavorable result. Read the instructions carefully and follow them.

**Product Tip #2:** Use product for at least three months.
Don't start using a new product and jump ship after using it unless you have an allergic reaction. I suggest giving a product at least three months to determine its effectiveness. However, if you find that using the product is causing your hair to suffer an immense amount of breakage, thinning, or loss, all bets are off.

**Product Tip #3:** Compare two products at once.

If you want to know which conditioner may work better on your hair, apply them on opposite sides of your head and test using comparison testing.

**Product Tip #4:** Use the entire product.

Before rushing off to buy a new product, just because someone else told you it was great, use the product you have. This will cut down on the amount of money you spend and will prevent you from becoming a product junkie. Try the "Use it All" method, and this will help you evaluate the products you currently have—without adding more to the mix.

**Product Tip #5:** Use for a year and a half and trash.

I trash my products after a year and a half of use. A rule of thumb is that all unopened products have a three-year shelf life. However, that time frame is decreased by half the moment you open the bottle and the product is used. To increase the product shelf life, handle your products with clean hands. Managing products with dirty hands or allowing others to do so will result in contamination of your products and decrease their shelf life. I don't do dirty hands in my bottles.

I try my best to stick with what is working while being open to adding a new product only after I've learned about the ingredients. If an ingredient looks suspicious or the benefits of its usage are unknown, I don't use the product. If I can't pronounce it using my best college education skills, then it too isn't necessary for me to use. The product isn't for me if I can't answer simple questions, such as these:

1. What does the product say it will do?
2. Does the product contain ingredients to do what the product says it will do?
3. Is this product natural?

**Sources: BlackHairMedia; EWG Skin Deep; Google**

# Hair Transition Exercise #5:
## Ingredient Check

Become familiar with the ingredients in your products. You won't be able to get away from some of these ingredients. It will be your job to determine how active an ingredient is within your product based on exactly where it is listed.

Pull out all of your hair products (yes all of them), and take an inventory. Identify any of the ingredients listed in this chapter that you should avoid.

If it's within the top five to seven ingredients listed, be careful. However, if it appears towards the end, be cautious but know it's not as potent as it would have been if it were listed higher on the list.

How many products did you find that contain ingredients on the "Ingredients to Avoid" list?

# Of Products:_____

"No fear formed against me shall prosper."

—DIANA RAMSEY

# 11 | #52Day Inspiration

No two fear breakdowns are created equal.

They will all look different and make those living in fear experience different reactions. My fear looked like avoidance, perfectionism, lack of sleep, and eventually, my emotional breakdown.

I kept saying I was good, but the lie was that I had been living in fear for an entire year. But I wasn't good when I boxed up all of the jewelry along with my plans for releasing it and threw everything in the basement.

I had moved on from the pain, but one day I went looking for something in the basement and found my fears staring back at me saying, "We're still here."

## Fear Had Won

Although my breakdown seemed to come out of nowhere, it had its roots in how my focus group feedback made me feel. The first night, I cried. I was in mourning over the things I had let stop me, scare me out of flying, and inevitably, keep me stagnant. Two more nights passed before I told someone I wasn't feeling like myself. An entire week went by before I informed my mother something wasn't right with me. That was probably the first time my family ever heard "Diana isn't doing well." They had grown up knowing I was always all right, but not this time.

I wasn't going to disregard my emotional state so everyone could feel okay. I learned in that moment that I was an enabler to many of my family and friends. I had maintained a facade of a person who always had it together and now they didn't know what to do to help me. Some did very well, but others either stopped talking to me during that time or just seemed uncomfortable and unsure of what to do or to say.

Two weeks passed, and I basically stopped running my business. I called out of work frequently during this time, but I still managed to get my work done and remain gainfully employed.

It wasn't until my friend Julian B. Kiganda, of Bold & Fearless, invited me to one of her monthly parties that I even left my house. I had been telling her I would attend for a while and felt bad I had yet to make good on that promise, so I went. I didn't want to put on a face and act like I was okay, so I didn't; I got dressed and was simply there.

The event kicked off with an amazing talk from Mocha Ochoa-Nana, a successful literary publicist, and I was happy I decided to attend. My spirits had been raised, and being in such great company quieted my tears of sadness. Before leaving the party, I decided to purchase the Bold & Fearless Quote Cards, not thinking much about how they would play a role in my life. I didn't get home before opening the pack in the car and flipping over the first card. It read:

*"Fear & faith cannot live in the same place."*

Wow. Someone had read my diary because this was exactly how I had been feeling. I was living in fear, so my faith was shot.

My initial instinct wasn't to jump on Periscope (a live video broadcast platform) and talk about the quote card, but I had to tell someone why reading a card with such a powerful message had caused me to act. My decision to get on Periscope was really just me sitting in my room the next day and saying, "Oh, what the hell! What do I have to lose?" I did my very first Periscope video, and in the middle of the conversation, I said "I'll pull a card tomorrow and come back to tell you the impact it had on my day." It was just that simple.

#52DayInspiration was born.

Being in a dark place filled with fear opens you to thoughts and things you would have never allowed around you. I knew my life wasn't meant to be the way I was living it. Fear couldn't win, but I had to get my faith up. Surprisingly, there were others like me on Periscope, people willing to tune in to my live broadcast every day. Every day wasn't beautiful; it was hard, and possibly the hardest thing I've done to date.

For the first time since starting SistersWithBeauty in 2011, I wasn't trying to wow people with my hairstyles to avoid showing them the real me; I just wanted to get better. I didn't realize the impact the cards were having on others and me until possibly day 20. I was allowing the quote cards to pull me out of my despair. I knew I was drowning, but it's hard to ask someone to save you from yourself if you don't first recognize you need help and are worth saving.

Once Julian heard how I was using her quote cards to pull me out of my state of mind, she joined in on the Periscopes to enhance the conversation. By day 35, I felt like I was swinging out from the darkness and into the light, but I didn't want to chance it by proclaiming I was all better without going the distance. The #ScopeFam (my nickname for the viewers) was amazing. They opened up their lives and screamed, "I feel the same way." They gave so much to the public process of my healing. By day 52, it was nothing but a party on-line, amongst family and friends. I had beaten fear with love, light, honesty, transparency, and most of all, *faith*.

After getting off that last #52DayInspiration call, I cried, but not the same tears I had shed fifty-two days prior. I was crying out of thanks for being worthy enough to be saved. Thinking back on the process of healing can still push me to tears. I've known people who ended their lives because they didn't tell someone they needed help. My own brother was possibly in an emotional depression and didn't know where to turn for help and answers. But I was alive because I did. The transition didn't break me, but it did give me a lot to think about in terms of my "what next?"

The funny thing about any transition you're in is that you will not be the same after it's over. Transitions are meant to be uncomfortable so you don't stay in your current state longer than you should. Your transition is about growing bigger wings so you can fly higher. But growth has pain, scars, and marks to prove it won't be easy and it hasn't been for me.

"One can be confused,
but you must never
stay confused."

—DIANA RAMSEY

# 12 | Natural Hair Terminology

"I BC'd and had a TWA for 6 months but after doing Protective Styles I was BSL by the end of a year."

The above sentence is an example of what happens to many Butterflies returning to their natural hair.

These were the type of conversations people would have right in front of me or in hair chats. It had to be one of my least favorite things about the natural hair community, mainly because I didn't know what they were talking about and I felt left out. One of the most intimidating factors in the natural hair community is learning new terminology and acronyms. The natural hair community (NHC) has a style all of its own. It seemed like every day a new word was being added to the long list of other words that I didn't understand how to use or what they meant.

I started to write down the meaning of every word or acronym I read or heard. Understanding and accepting that there were some words which were introduced but never stuck with me, I tried to at least understand the basics.

These words may have come across your screen, but sometimes the meaning of the words isn't always the same when they're used by different people.

Here is my list of natural hair terminology. Know that this list is not all encompassing, and even after this book is published, someone will probably make up new words just to spite me.

**Apple Cider Vinegar (ACV) Rinse:** Washing hair with vinegar to cleanse, condition, and remove bacteria. Used to make your hair shine and to treat dandruff. Rinsing with apple cider vinegar will help balance the pH of your hair and remove the buildup that can result from the use of styling products and inexpensive shampoos.

**Bagging:** Placing a plastic cap on your hair (dry or wet) for duration of thirty minutes to overnight. This is done to restore moisture to the hair.

**Bag-Bag-Conditioning Cap-Towel (BBCT):** Effective way of generating heat to your hair if you don't sit under a physical dryer or use a handheld blow-dryer. BBCT method is used during Deep Conditioning (DC) or other treatments to the hair.

**Big Chop (BC):** The cutting of all relaxed hair. When an individual BCs, it is the most significantly documented time of a Natural's life. It is the shedding of an old idea and the growth of a new image. (I like to call this the Butterfly Chop.)

**Borrowing Hair:** During your twists you take from one side of hair to make up for the lack in the other side of hair. This creates a longer, more complicated time untwisting, and it can result in knots if untwisted incorrectly. Don't borrow hair.

**Coily:** The hair texture classification of many women with natural hair. This texture resembles a spring or spiral and is most often visible when hair is wet.

**Co-Wash/No Poo:** Washing hair with conditioner to avoid the harsh cleansers found in shampoos. SWB does not recommend this method.

**Creamy Crack:** A term used to refer to a chemical relaxer.

**Deep Condition (DC):** Leaving a moisturizing conditioner on your hair for an extended amount of time. To increase penetration, sit under a hooded dryer.

**Hair Length Goals:** The hair length a Natural aspires to reach. The following terms all describe hair length goals.

- Neck Length (NL)
- Shoulder Length (SL)
- Arm Pit Length (APL)
- Bra Strap Length (BSL)
- Waist Length (WL)
- Hip Length (HL)
- Tail Bone Length (TBL)

**Liquid, Oil, Cream (LOC) Method:** The sequence in which you apply these products (liquid, oil, and cream) to your hair that is believed to result in moisture retention and shine.

**No Heat Zone:** Refraining from applying heat to your hair.

**Pineapple:** A type of sleeping hairstyle to preserve your hair for the next day. This style is achieved on longer hair. An individual gathers up all of her hair in a loose ponytail at the very top of her head, wraps hair in a satin bonnet. In the morning, the ponytail is removed and her curls are preserved for styling.

**Product Junkie** (PJ): An individual who obsessively buys hair products.

**Teeny Weeny Afro (TWA):** A small Afro often worn after cutting off the remainder of a relaxer.

**Transitioning:** Allowing the natural hair to grow while maintaining the chemically processed ends in order to avoid a dramatic cut.

**Twist Out:** Two-strand twists, dried by air or a low setting dryer and undone for styling.

**Wash and Go:** Washing your hair, letting it air dry, and doing minimum to no styling.

# Hair Transition Exercise #6:
## Natural Hair Sentence

Make up a natural hair sentence using at least three words from this chapter. Now you should be better equipped to understand natural hair conversations. So go ahead and BC to get your TWA, then DC and hit up a mean Twist out. Okay?

_____

_____

_____

_____

_____

_____

_____

_____

_____

_____

_____

_____

_____

_____

_____

_____

"Free your mind from the trappings of fear so you can get your light."

—DIANA RAMSEY

# 13 | Evict Your Fear

Fear is not a place where you should lay your bags down and set up a residence to live comfortably. Fear is supposed to act as your opposition to challenge you to continue to move forward. It should be your tug-of-war opponent so that, in the end, you are announced as the winner. But I'm no different from anyone who has been a coward in the face of her fears. I've let fear win many of my battles.

The eviction of fear was not only a choice but also an action to push me out of living in it. I had become comfortable with not doing the things I said I wanted to do because no one was holding me accountable to getting them done, not even me.

Fear is a topic that deserves its own top billing, center stage, and spotlight. During #52DayInspiration I realized how much power I had given my fears. I was afraid to release jewelry I'd spent hours, days, and months learning how to make. I was afraid to release Bet It All on Black to an audience and ask anyone for help in launching that idea. I was afraid to talk about anything other than hair because I felt people only wanted to see one skill set from me. I was afraid to cut my hair because I thought it would limit my ability to attract people to me and to my blog.

I had given fear all of that space and energy to grow and inevitably keep me in my own personal darkness.

We all do this, or we've all done this, at some point in our lives. Something seems hard or isn't given to us the way we thought it would be, and suddenly we become scared of it, conceding to the idea that we should have never tried it in the first place.

Fear is only as strong as we make it, but in the eye of the storm, I can't tell my left from my right. I didn't see my way out of the fear, so I built walls and locked doors to its existence. But it got bigger, and soon I had to tackle the tenant who never paid rent but took up more space than I did.

I'm learning how to fear less, but make no mistake about it, I'm not fear free. Right now I'm telling my fears to people who are strong enough to recognize and understand them and push me to do it afraid. That's been my biggest lesson. To tell someone else you're afraid is necessary because each person's fears are not the same and you need someone who isn't afraid of what's on the other side to help you get there. All of my life, I've been so independent; this is uncharted water for me. I work every day at trying to not be so afraid that I fail to tell my fears to people who can help. That's a whole new challenge in itself.

Fear isn't something you grow out of overnight, and it doesn't mean, because I've tackled my fear of releasing my jewelry and sold out of the same pieces a group of seven women found childish, that I'm over my fears for good. However, I'm over those particular fears and have pictures of happy customers wearing their Butterfly jewelry to prove it.

I've learned that my fears only held up the people I was supposed to help with my story and my actions.

It has been important to speak my fears out loud and give them an eviction notice. A fear I will have tackled by the time this book is released is the fear of cutting my hair.

I spent two years seeing amazing cuts splashed all over social media. Naturals who were known for having long hair were either cutting it all off or shaving the sides and keeping the top a little longer. To say I loved this look was an understatement. This style was just the style I could see myself wearing and adding my own flare to, but I simply continued to be afraid of carrying out the cut. I stayed stuck between wanting to cut my hair and fearing the cut far too long. When I sat down to evaluate why I was afraid, I came up with this list of reasons why cutting my hair scared me:

- It could limit me with my styling options.
- I may not like it.
- I may regret my decision.
- Followers may not like it.
- Followers may stop following me for hair tips and styles.
- I may altogether hate the look.
- It could mess up my brand.
- My career could be affected.

This list of potential negative results from cutting my hair continued to grow. My fears were birthing uncertainty and paranoia that didn't have a leg to stand on but had power over me to convince me not to cut my hair. The crazy thing about fear is that all you have to do is believe in the things that scare you and they will always hold power over you.

In order to evict my fears, I first had to know what they were. So I wrote each one down along with one action step to start the process of living fearlessly. I wanted the haircut and came to the conclusion that *I* was the only reason why I wasn't rocking the style I loved. My memories of what long hair once meant to me played in my mind and continued to affect me, but how long could I stay in that place?

I put the first plan to cut my hair in motion by simply telling someone I wanted to do it. Next, I asked friends to recommend a barber, and before I knew it, there wasn't anything hard about planning to do what I wanted to do. To cut my hair and free myself of my childhood beliefs that I wasn't enough without long hair was exactly what I needed.

I found out how easy it was to live more fearlessly in making decisions like this to change the way I had been thinking.

I was evicting fear, one step at a time.

"The caterpillar and butterfly know how to be patient. It's the only way you grow."

—DIANA RAMSEY

# 14 | Patience, Determination & Fun

**Patience:** noun. Bearing provocation, annoyance, misfortune, delay, hardship, pain, etc., with fortitude and calm and without complaint, anger, or the like. (dictionary.com)

**Determination:** noun. A quality that makes you continue trying to do or achieve something that is difficult. (merriam-webster.com)

**Fun:** adjective. Someone or something that is amusing or enjoyable: (merriam-webster.com)

I needed patience to get through my transition, I needed determination to see me through the days when I wanted to give up, and I needed fun to experience the newness of my natural hair journey. In order for me to return to my natural hair, I had to be open to experiencing all three of these things.

Patience is understanding that Rome wasn't built in a day and neither was my natural hair journey. I'm still learning how to be patient after five years. There have been days when my hair frustrated me to the point where I just wanted to quit. What I noticed about those who did actually quit was that they didn't fully understand the three things that needed to happen during their journey in order for it to be successful. I remember being in the bathroom crying because I couldn't flat twist my own hair, but I wasn't trying to learn either, so I was caught in a cycle of frustration fueled by my inability. During this time, activating patience is how I got over my issue with flat twists.

Determination is another story. Even today, I have to remain fixed on the things I want to do. Making up your mind and being committed to see yourself through your natural hair journey will be your biggest test. While many admire the natural hair look, feel, and style, a small few are not determined enough to do the work required to achieve it. I had to ask myself if I was one of those people. Was I determined enough to see my natural hair journey to the end? I faced this question in my hair and life transitions. : We always have the option to check yes or no with many of our decisions.

☐ Yes                    ☐ No

If you select no, that's cool, and you can now move on to things you really do want to do. If you answer yes, then you continue down the road to the next lesson. I'm starting to see life is just that simple, but it's made difficult when our answer is neither yes nor no. You have to choose.

Fun is what I've learned to lean on when I'm having bad hair days or things just are not working in my favor. The discovery of my hair texture, creating new styles, and engagement with the natural hair community have all provided a great backdrop of fun memories. The moment when I embraced my natural hair the most was during a time I was having fun showing other Naturals how quickly I could style my hair. I had to learn how to embrace my natural hair and have fun styling. I wouldn't be writing books, shooting and editing videos, and managing www.sisterswithbeauty.com if I didn't have fun doing it. But that doesn't say every day is awesome or will be the most amazing; it just means my overall experience has been enjoyable and pleasant.

Patience, determination, and fun are the fibers that bind and strengthen the threads of your natural hair journey. To this day I still keep them near as constant reminders that this should be a good experience for not only my hair but my life as well. Otherwise, what do I have to look forward to?

## Hair Transition Exercise #7:
## I'm returning to my natural hair because...

This is the time to be transparent with yourself.

I'm returning to my natural hair because: (fill in the blanks below).

_____

_____

_____

_____

_____

_____

_____

_____

_____

_____

_____

_____

_____

_____

_____

_____

"To free yourself, you have to finally let go of what's been holding onto you."

—DIANA RAMSEY

# 15 | Disappearing Acts

At one point, I discovered a similarity between my father and the men I dated. Truth is it was kind of sad and not something I realized until dating in my 30's. I dated men who exhibited the same disappearing act as my father—opting to vanish without a single word, no goodbye, not even a warning when they left that they would never return.

I can recall three men I really wanted to be with who disappeared out of my life with no trace and no expectation that they planned to return. It made me wonder about love and my ability to fall into its lap.

In my thirties I didn't foresee myself experiencing the disappearing acts of my past, but it was like these men found me just to carry out these actions, or at least that's how I was beginning to feel.

The story went like this. I would meet a man who persistently gained my trust and attention, and then without warning, he would disappear without a reason for our dating demise.

I was left crushed far past what I believed to be normal sadness. I could never wrap my mind around how one day we were good and the next day we were done. Each time, it left me with a series of questions. What had I done wrong? What happened? Was he okay? And why couldn't he just be a man and tell me? These questions spun around my head, forcing me into a deeper sadness, until I filled up my day with things to do or new interests grabbed my attention. The intense feeling of wanting to know why never left my side, even as another disappeared on me. Sometimes people can do things so deeply rooted into your past that you hold on to those people out of fear of having to finally let go of what's been holding on to you.

My most recent disappearing act experience sent me into this same spiral of sadness, but I wasn't the same as I had been during the previous occurrences. I was finally able to place why I had the reaction that I did; it was the emotional distress of someone picking up and leaving me that made me feel so down. The abrupt ending made me feel stuck, as if someone told me to stand in one spot and never move again. I felt hopeless to love, to date, or to even meet new prospects. I realized I still had not come to grips with the actions of my father.

That last disappearing act sent me into an emotional breakdown that I didn't try to avoid with business plans and things to do. This emotional purge was long overdue. I was finally crying over Ronnie, my dad, letting go of twenty years of pain stored up and never before released. I had avoided the emotional side of losing my father and my brother all in one fell swoop. I was finally in a place to deal with the grieving and loss.

In experiencing this ah-ha moment in my life, I'm starting to see all of the walls I've built up around me out of the need to protect myself from pain. I'm heavily guarded against pain, and it's not how I wanted to be as much as how I came to be. But finally, I stood in front of my life mirror and admitted some of my hardest truths to myself. I needed to work on forgiveness and moving forward for my own sanity. I had to learn the importance of letting go and moving on and allowing people to come or go without needing to know the why behind their leaving.

My need to control every aspect of my life was a result of not being able to control things that hurt me. I couldn't control the decision my brother made to take his life, nor could I control the fact that my father disappeared as a result.

Those two very traumatic occurrences happened at the same time, and I had never dealt with them.

We are not what happens to us or what we choose to hold on to.

Realizing this fact is finally allowing me to let go.

"I give myself permission
to become."

—DIANA RAMSEY

# 16 | Confidently Transitioning

How do I transition confidently? I asked this question internally, before, during, and after returning to my natural hair. Not everyone will have confidence issues, but that doesn't mean they can't and won't surface when you're faced with certain situations during your transition.

Returning to your natural hair will not automatically make you confident. It's important to assess your confidence, because cutting off all of your hair can test your confidence and belief in yourself more than you can imagine. I experienced this when I cut off all of my hair. Making dramatic changes in the person you've been can weigh heavily on the person you will become. During this time, I leaned on what I knew to be true about myself to get over humps, dings, and bumps in my confidence. Negative comments, bad hair days, and slow hair growth can all play a part in the way you feel and the way you view yourself.

Being confident is a feeling.

Although I felt confident going into my journey, there were times when I didn't always feel the most beautiful. Admitting this doesn't make me or you a horrible person or a person who lacks love for herself. It makes us both real and able to have a conversation that doesn't always place us in the best light.

Sometimes you may wake up and just not feel anything good. We've all had times when we didn't feel our best, but during those times, I also had to recognize the facts and try to pull myself back up. I've done the following to keep my confidence up or to pick myself back up when I've fallen short.

**Tip #1:** See the positive in yourself.
Identify one amazing thing about yourself every day, and block out any negative thoughts. Negativity distracts you from seeing your own beauty.

**Tip #2:** Write yourself a love letter.
This one might sound crazy, but write it anyway. When you can verbally express the love you have for yourself, you can read the words aloud and receive them in a loving and fulfilling way.

**Tip #3:** Wear an outfit you know is a showstopper.
The best way to get a confidence boost is to wear something you already know results in you feeling great.

**Tip #4:** Treat yourself.
Do something to pamper yourself. This can be a nice hot bath, a pedicure and manicure, or a full-on spa day. No matter what you choose, allow it to be something that ties directly into relaxation and personal pleasure. Sometimes the intimate moments you have with yourself are the real keys to increasing your self-confidence.

**Tip #5:** Greet yourself in the mirror as "Beautiful."
Words hold a lot of meaning and importance in how we view ourselves. Talking positively about your own reflection in the mirror is a great way to boost your confidence.

We all have to become our own cheerleaders and hype squad. Seeing myself adorned with my natural hair for the first time was a shocker. I didn't realize how unique my look really was because my hair had always been my focus.

Sure, I had days when I wanted to blame how I felt on my hair, but I really had to get down to the simple truth. I wasn't created perfectly, and any flaws I noticed were perfectly placed there for me to love and learn to accept. Transitioning confidently was something I never knew needed be talked about, but it does. This is due to the image of confidence women exude once they return to their natural hair. It all seems to be automatic. In order to go confidently into your natural hair journey, you must be willing to accept yourself as you are, and when that becomes difficult, you just have more work to do to discover your beauty.

I began combating my days of low confidence with words to lift me up. After choosing about fifteen words that I used to push me into a better place, I used them as a way to build myself up while transitioning. It helped me on those days when I woke up not feeling my best. No one can escape occasionally feeling like you're not enough or don't have enough. On those days, you have to be able to use whatever you can to pull yourself out of that despair and into a new way of thinking. In your hair or life journey, that's all you can do. Try your best to maintain healthy thoughts about your self image.

# Hair Transition Exercise #8:
## IAMSWB

Pick 3-5 words from the **#IAMSWB** Butterfly that you feel give you strength. Write them down on a sticky note and place them on the mirror in your bathroom. Every day, read your words aloud before going outside. Store up all of the positive energy from your words, and let it carry you through your day. This is what I did to build up my confidence on days when it was questionable. Place things in your home that build you up and help support you into tomorrow.

Beautiful • Confident • Determined • Encouraging • Focused • Fly • Free • Inspiring
Intelligent • Leader • Motivating • Successful • Powerful • Strong • Stylish

"The only time growing stops is when you're no longer moving."

—DIANA RAMSEY

# 17 | Transition Never Stops

I wanted to return to my natural hair, and that was it. There was no groundbreaking epiphany in making that decision, at least not in the beginning. My transition has been filled with lessons, blessings, milestones, and growth. The real question was whether or not my hair transition had anything to do with how my life was unfolding and changing.

I personally believe my hair had a tremendous impact on my life.

My hair transition changed the way I allowed others to view me. In the beginning, I tried to be perfect. As I continued to face my fears, I realized I needed to just be human and live my life.

I'm learning how my life can be of service to someone else. How I can have more of an impact and contribute my gifts and purpose to others.

I'm no longer trying to hide from myself; I'm now allowing people to see all of me. I'm not perfect, having my fear breakdown proved that, but it also helped me to see that we are supposed to continue to transition because it never stops. Had I never gone on my hair journey, I can't be sure I would have been open to doing the real work to change my life. I had to become comfortably uncomfortable, no longer content to stay the person I was, and finally excited about the person I was to become.

The biggest secret you'll discover after you officially transition your hair is that your life will always be in transition. You'll always be in a Butterfly Transition, just in different forms. Sure, my transition started with my hair, as yours possibly did too, but that's not where this story or your story ends. I am evolving, always changing, sculpting, and rearranging. So are you.

I've learned a few lessons, related to both hair and life, that in sharing with you I gift back to myself.

## Hair & Life Transition Lessons

1. You are meant to break down the walls so that people can see you as you are and not as they want you to be.

2. No matter what, God loves you and has a job for you to do.

3. You don't have to fold into anyone's ideas of what you should be. #BeYourBeauty

4. You control your happiness or unhappiness.

5. You only repeat the same mistakes when you don't learn the lesson the first time.

6. If you give fear a name, food, and a place to stay, it will continue to live because you say so.

7. As long as you have life, you have purpose.

Before picking up this book, it's possible you only thought about how you could make your hair transition better, but now that you've turned enough pages, start thinking about your life and how it is transitioning too. This is the best time to allow them both to grow in harmony together. Become sensitive to what you can stand to learn from both of them. It took me almost five years to realize my hair and life were in transition together.

As my hair grew, so did I, even when I wasn't paying attention.

As I made bad hair-care decisions, the same decisions were being made in my life.

As I found triumph in a successful twist out, my life pulled toward that same triumphant reality. I needed to decide the best way to move forward and when I felt strong enough cutting off the old for the new.

The bridge between my hair and my life transitions has saved my life and put me on a new path of discovery. I don't want to simply be known for fierce hairstyles. In my past, I've used the ability to style my hair as a way to keep strangers away from me and leave those who know me to wonder exactly who I am.

With my current understanding of how my hair and life are making a new way for me, I no longer want to distract you from getting to know the real me.

"It's okay to have Butterflies; that means you are invested in doing the work."

—DIANA RAMSEY

# 18 | Having Second Thoughts?

Have you returned to your natural hair only to find you're having second thoughts? What is it? Too hard? Styles not looking how you expected? Still unsure what products to use on your hair? Or better yet, your hair isn't what you expected it to be?

You've read books and watched countless YouTube videos, and none of them talked about what to do when you lose interest or are not living with the natural hair of your dreams. Second thoughts happen to many of us, so you're not alone; I had them pop out of nowhere sporadically when things were not going as I expected. It was always important for me to find the root cause of my second thought syndrome (STS). I had to be honest with myself during the moments when I wanted to throw in the towel.

Once I admitted what it was that caused me to have second thoughts, I then had to ask myself why I was letting those thoughts infiltrate my mind.

I couldn't remember the last time I hadn't second-guessed myself. I noticed I second-guessed my decisions more when I didn't know the outcome or true benefit of what I was doing. The root cause of your second-guessing will have to be identified by you, just like I had to find the origins of my own.

It's natural to want to ensure you're making the right decision; that's why I'm always over-evaluating my decisions. We all just want to make the right decision without having to have hindsight help us out.

As an adult, the best guide you'll have towards making better decisions is to question the decisions you've already made. The healthy part about life is that we get to choose and question everything. In the end, it all boils down to us making a decision and either sticking with it or finding out the details to determine if it's truly meant for us.

I second-guessed writing this book. I still don't know what the true outcome of putting together a book such as this will be, but if I'd stayed in that moment of doubt, I would have never released this book to figure out its impact.

So don't be ashamed of having second thoughts. My best advice for you during that moment is to identify why you are reconsidering your decision. Answering the "3W" questions may also be helpful:

- Who is having second thoughts? (Internal or external influences)
- What do you think caused the second thoughts?
- Where do you wish to go from here?

When you can answer these questions, you'll come to a better conclusion about the root of your second-guessing. You'll hear many people say, "Natural hair isn't for everyone." This line is normally followed by reasons as to why many will not return to their natural hair. If that applies to you, that's totally fine. Just be able to clearly identify why you're no longer willing to complete your journey. Being honest with yourself may shed light on what is holding you back and potentially help you to move past it. Some of my best decisions to date have occurred from my honesty in saying exactly why I'm opposing my next move.

We would all be lying if we didn't admit there was a moment during our Butterfly Transition when we questioned, became afraid, and wanted to flee our journey, if even for a millisecond. In the end, if you don't believe in why you're transitioning and see no reason to continue, you can always quit or evaluate why you started in the first place. Sometimes going back to the reason you began your transition helps you continue.

# Hair Transition Exercise #9:
## Second Thoughts Questionnaire

If you're currently questioning your natural hair journey, I want you to answer the following questions:

1. Why did you want to return to your natural hair?

_____

_____

2. What is bothering you about your natural hair?

_____

_____

3. Why do you want to stop your transition journey?

_____

_____

"You can't miss what you never had ... but I do."

—DIANA RAMSEY

# 19 | Dear Daddy

People bank on the phrase, "you can't miss what you never had." I denounce this notion because I know it wasn't true for me. The one thing I always wanted to tell my dad was:

"I lived; I survived; I did not die."

I always felt robbed of my innocence by a past I never fully understood. While my mother instilled her strength in me, I poured myself a glass of my father's absence. I drank from the fountain of "poor little black girl who has no father."

During a conversation, a friend told me I dodged a bullet when my father left my life, but I rejected this notion. In my past, I would have accepted this as a fact, but on that day, it wasn't going to be the hope I would cling to. I wanted my father in my life, as he should have been. I didn't feel like I had dodged a bullet. I felt like a bus hit me when I was already falling.

Our conversation made me want to tell my father, who had been absent over twenty years, about all of my frustrations, emotions, wants, and needs, and so I did. There was nothing stopping me from releasing the emotional hold I was finally able to say had been holding me back.

*Dear Ronnie Pigram,*

*Can you count how many performances you missed? I can. I calculated them in roses or flowers all the other performers received from their fathers.*

*I tried to find you. Realizing I never knew your whole truth sent me on a wild goose chase with no end in sight. My start became my finish, but maybe I gave up too soon. Maybe I am just like you.*

*Dear Daddy,*

*I feared one day I'd find you on the outskirts of my own hurt. Run and hug you, no, stand still and stare at you until you disappeared, again. Alive? I've never known. Happy? I wondered how. I've only had uncertainty for you in my soul. While succeeding at many things, I've often felt as if I were standing still.*

*I never mourned the absence of you. It wasn't until I broke down completely, in my thirties, that I had to face what had never been. The shadow of my past, the man I barely knew. You.*

*Dear Daddy,*

*I would die one thousand times if someone stopped me on the street claiming I looked like you. I've never seen a woman on your side of the family to know what she would look like. I'm hardly healed from my pain; only able to consider your absence a factor that has plagued me greatly. I wonder if you would have stayed if I were your son. Time has tried to patch my pain, but time can never do. I still wonder, where are you?*

*If anyone has ever seen or met Ronnie Pigram, they should know I'm looking for you. I'll pray for your salvation and for my forgiveness too. For in the end of the days of our lives, I'll know you miss me too.*

*The daughter you never knew,*

*—Diana*

The writing of *Butterfly Transition* made me confront some of my biggest hurts and disappointments. As I wrote, exposing chapters about my hair and life, I began to talk more and more about my father. Sharing stories with my closest friends that they had never heard me tell. Until one day, two friends asked me in the same week:

"Do you want to try to look for him again?"

The first time, I avoided the question. The second time, I couldn't deny my interest. I did want to try to look for him again. But knowing this time I would have friends helping me made me feel as if I was going to actually get closure.

My first time searching was in 2010, when I moved to Texas. I woke up one day and proclaimed, "I'm going to find my father." But my search brought out emotions I wasn't ready to deal with. Instead of continuing my search, I moved forward with a wonderful idea to start a website called SistersWithBeauty. Now I'm back where I started. No matter what I discover, I plan on going the distance this time.

**Biological Father:** Ronnie E. Pigram

**Last Residence:** Harvey, Illinois

**Living:** Unknown

I don't know what this part of my Butterfly Transition holds, but I'm ready to find out. No matter what I discover, it won't change my past of hurt and disappointment. It could possibly bring more hurt and pain my way, but I don't believe God would have me on any path to watch me self-destruct.

I'm looking for my father;

I'm cutting my hair;

I'm becoming fearless;

I'm living out my Butterfly Transition.

"On the other side of
your Butterfly Transition
are bigger wings."

—DIANA RAMSEY

# 20 | Life After the Transition

So what does life look like after your transition?

Well, in my opinion, the answer will be up to you, me, and how we choose to go about living out the lessons our transition has shown us.

After you've learned all you need to know, the next thing to do is begin to implement and navigate.

Your transition will be everything you allow it to be. You may even have the same epiphany I had. If I could be so dedicated to my hair and all of its changes, I could apply that same care and consideration to my life.

I'm finding that I can, and it's important for me to keep going in this direction. I'm no longer the person interested in only giving you hair advice. I know I was meant for so much more than just where to place a flat twist to make you feel beautiful. Sure, I want to step out looking amazing, but not at the expense of avoiding issues in my life.

This is my Butterfly Transition. I'm getting bigger wings.

I intend to learn more about my hair and, in turn, allow it to help shine light on my life.

Releasing the stories I've held on to for so long is helping me get my power back and turn the corner to healing.

My ongoing work with my transition is about being vulnerable and knowing that there is strength in being in that position.

I never truly knew what vulnerability meant, nor how it looked, but I'm learning. I feel the difference and see the difference, and it's even becoming noticeable to others. The voice I've been silencing out of fear is starting to speak loudly, and there is so much more growth coming my way.

To transition—there was a time when I thought this word only meant changing my hair, but it has taken on new meaning.

**Butterfly Transition:** noun. The process of constantly growing in and out of your current life, decisions, moods, position, and purpose, and into the person you (are to become) were always meant to become.

I pray my lessons, and even the uncomfortable memories I've shared, help to allow you to find your way through your own hair and life transition.


Bless up, and fly high.

Diana

## Hair Transition Exercise #10:
## Capture Life after Your Transition

Keep track of all your experiences through pictures and journaling. Take pictures of your good days, bad days, and anything that you want to share or capture. Remember it's not just your hair that will grow and change, but your life will too. Never stop celebrating your growth, your light, your transition. Use the journal in your book to capture exactly where you are in your life. Write down what's on your mind and don't spare yourself from your own truth. Remember, it is in your truth that you are set free. Let's start doing the work today.

_____

_____

_____

_____

_____

_____

_____

_____

_____

_____

_____

_____

# Notes

_____

_____

_____

_____

_____

_____

_____

_____

_____

_____

_____

_____

_____

_____

_____

_____

_____

_____

_____

_____

# Notes

# BUTTERFLY TRANSITION

Original poem by Diana Ramsey
Written for your Butterfly Transition


My Butterfly Transition,
My fears, my secrets, my life, my hair, my future,

They were all staring me in the face,
Asking when I was going to give them their day in the sun.

Then I broke.

I'd spent so much time being an outward motivator
To anyone in my path, but it was me who lacked motivation.

I tried to pour out my empty cup, wondering why it was never enough.
I was in a Butterfly Transition
The moment between being comfortably uncomfortable and purely terrified
of change.
Butterfly Transition
Between knowing you can't stay where you are and fearing where you're
supposed to be.

My butterfly transition

Between motivating you on conscious hair decisions and giving my life the
attention that it needs

I am in my Butterfly Transition.
I realized it like a slow playback of a movie I had yet to see or hear anyone
talk about.
To transition,
Only used in my vocabulary to describe the difference between relaxing my
hair and not.

Shea butter and olive oil or neutralizing shampoo and petroleum,
Those were the only transitions I'd come to know.
The child pulling at my leg annoyed every fiber of my being.
I didn't have children and had not planned on birthing any in this lifetime.

But that child was truth, and to say I wanted to sit down in a room full of my own fears and give labor to the reality of their existence was the farthest from my mind—

My hair transition made me more conscious about how I decided care for my hair,

But what about my life?

I stored away stories and past pains, fears, losses and gains, only showing the most finished element of myself,
My hair.

Imagine the amount of time spent on a hairstyle only meant to wow you away from the person wearing it.

I've been this person for so long it seems legit.
My authenticity to be me was never in question, but being true isn't about not being fake.

It's about making decisions and living loudly in them.

My Butterfly Transition
Won't look like yours, it won't feel like it, and surely isn't meant to make the same decisions you will or move the same as I have.

But you too are in transition.

The line between coming, staying, and going.
Crying, smiling, or knowing, fearing, exciting, or holding on to the person you now fear; the person you will become is far too foreign to imagine.

Your Butterfly Transition is supposed to make you uncomfortable, your breathing is supposed to be short, the space you're in is supposed to be tight because on the other side of your Butterfly Transition are bigger wings.

Big enough to carry you out of your transition and into a new reality.

Coco Chanel said a woman who cuts her hair is about to change her life.

I've always seen this statement as incomplete.
Sure she is about to change her life, but how many more lives can she change if she tells people why she's doing it?
How they can take that same strength and apply it to their lives? How that insignificant cut is making an exceptional change in her life.

I sat on the sidelines of fear, wanting to be and do so much more than I was doing at the time.

I played myself for small.

I clipped my wings and forgot I could fly.

Butterfly Transition is about constantly growing in and out of your current life, decisions, moods, position, and purpose.

And into the person you are to become.

I found myself in my Butterfly Transition,

Both in my hair and my

Life.

# I'S NATURAL NOW

Original poem by Diana Ramsey.
Written for your Hair Transition.

I's Natural now
Come look and see
See why all these people staring at me
I's Natural now, so that means I can be true
To the person looking back at me in the mirror, and it ain't you
I's Natural now, so I can do as I please
Don't need your opinion or your nasty looks, looking down upon me
I's Natural now, and you can say what you like
But no one stares you down from head to toe when you come in sight
I's Natural now
I'm standing so tall, without a care in the world, nope, not one at all
I's Natural now
Oh, you don't like my hair? Then turn the hell around, and I still won't care
I's Natural now, and I did it just for me
I'm flying and soaring and twisting for free
I's Natural now my transition is here
I can see me as me and have nothing to fear
I's Natural
I'm Free
A Slave to no one, not even me
I's Natural Now
I AM
ME...

# BUTTERFLY TRANSITION SPOKEN WORD

**Visit www.sisterswithbeauty.com/btsw to watch the full spoken word video.**

"BUTTERFLY TRANSITION"
A SPOKEN WORD TRACK BY
*Diana Ramsey*

Sisters With Beauty®
sisterswithbeauty.com

# DID YOU ENJOY?

Reviews are one of the best ways to help other readers find *Butterfly Transition*. Somewhere another Butterfly is looking to get her wings. If you enjoyed the book, felt it helped you in your hair or life transition, please leave a review with one of the following *Butterfly Transition* book-selling sites.

- SistersWithBeauty.com
- Amazon.com
- BarnesandNoble.com

# RESOURCES

I'm happy to share my sources used to create the
*Butterfly Transition* book.

Research—Black Hair Media
blackhairmedia.com

EWG Skin Deep
www.ewg.org

Branding & Design—Julian B. Kiganda
www.julianbkiganda.com

Photography—E.Y.E. Imagery
www.eye-imagery.com

Wardrobe & Styling—TheStyleMedic
www.thestylemedic.com

Hairstyling & Barbering—Yoko
@TheYokoProject

Lesley "Lady Clipper"
@LadyClipper

Make Up Artist—Danni "FaceValue Artistry"
@FVArtisty

# ABOUT THE AUTHOR

**DIANA RAMSEY:** Founder and Beauty Empowerer of SistersWithBeauty, is an entrepreneur, motivator, and champion of confidence and sisterhood. Diana continues to use beauty as a way to empower women of color to celebrate, help, and empower themselves. Her passion is what drives Butterflies to the SistersWithBeauty.com daily. Diana leans on her Bachelor of Science degree in Business Entrepreneurship from Norfolk State University (c/o 2006) as she continues to build the SistersWithBeauty brand. She is a lover of dipping sauce, thrift shopping, and good vibe music.

Diana R. Ramsey, Beauty Empowerer:
www.sisterswithbeauty.com

# ABOUT THE COVER

**JULIAN B. KIGANDA:** is a dynamic branding and marketing strategist with nearly 20 years of experience helping transform, build and grow brands for international organizations, Fortune 500 corporations, multi-million dollar nonprofits and small businesses. She founded Bold & Fearless in 2013, an online magazine and lifestyle brand for professional women who are passionate discovering and living out their purpose. Julian is also an active public speaker and mentor and who has been featured in numerous media including ABC News, NBC News, The Washington Post, Essence.com, ARISE Magazine, Voice of America Africa and NPR.

Julian B. Kiganda Brand Consultancy
www.julianbkiganda.com

Bold & Fearless
www.boldandfearless.me

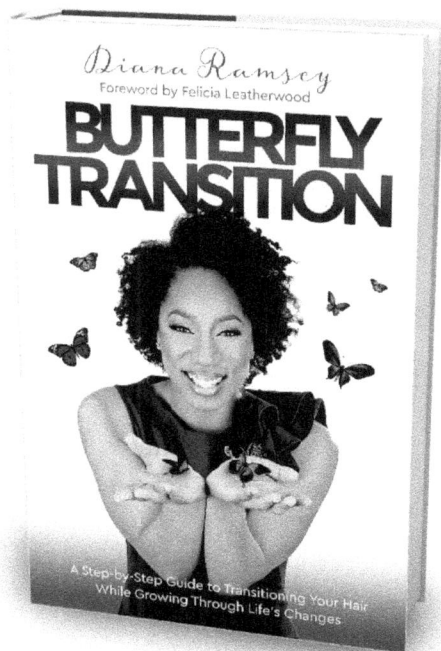

# ABOUT THE PHOTOGRAPHY

**CRYSTALE SPEARMAN:** Crystale is a wife, a mother of three, and a studio photographer. She is the owner and founder of E.Y.E. Imagery, a portrait boutique where she does all of the photography personally. At E.Y.E. Imagery, she specializes in photographing business owners and entrepreneurs. This includes speakers, celebrities, authors, motivators, stylists, artists, bloggers, chefs, bakers, and anyone else who has a brand to build and maintain.

Crystale Spearman, Photographer
www.eye-imagery.com

# ABOUT THE INTERIOR ILLUSTRATION

**DANA BLY:** Known for her funky unconventional illustrations and graphic design, Dana has a deep passion for design and colors. She is a self-taught designer who discovered her talent at a late age. While working in the corporate world, she has designed on the side and knew that one day she would own her design studio.

Dana Bly, Illustrator
www.pardonmyfro.com

# JOIN SISTERSWITHBEAUTY

Facebook
www.facebook.com/SistersWithBeauty

Instagram
www.instagram.com/SistersWithBeauty

Twitter
twitter.com/SisWithBeauty

Pinterest
www.pinterest.com/SisWithBeauty

# LIVE YOUR LIFE IN
# BEAUTY & LIGHT

www.sisterswithbeauty.com

www.ingramcontent.com/pod-product-compliance
Lightning Source LLC
Chambersburg PA
CBHW070043100426

42740CB00013B/2777